The rumblin' of a coach we soon did hear,
A dog-cart followed closely in the rear.
We soon were mounted in our several places,
A glorious group o' smilin', happy faces,
The piper tun'd his pipes an' loudly blew,
The drivers cracked their whips an' aff we flew.

– Alexander Robb.

– Picture by courtesy of Grampian Transport Museum.

Published by Keith Murray Publications,
46 Portal Crescent, Tillydrone, Aberdeen, Scotland. AB2 2SP
and
Aberdeen University Library, Queen Mother Library, Meston Walk, Aberdeen. AB9 2UE
First published 1989

Printed and Typeset by Halcon Printing Ltd., Stonehaven.

ISBN 1 870978 17 X

Acknowledgements

Mike Craig and Caroline Gilbert of the Aberdeen University photographic department for their skills in producing first class prints from the G.W.W. source.
A special thank you to Mary Murray of the Special Collections Department of Aberdeen University for her co-operation and encouragement.

Cover Designed by Mitchell Davidson, 1989.

George Washington Wilson Collection
Photographs marked *A.U.L.* in this book can be bought as high quality prints, made from the original negatives.
Enquiries: The G.W.W. Collection, Queen Mother Library, Tel. (0224) 272579.

Abbreviations

A.U.L.   Aberdeen University Library, George Washington Wilson Collection.
R.S.   Robert Smith.
A.C.   Author's Collection.

The vanished Chapel – see Page 63.

When G.W.W. stamped his initials on Royal Deeside

Robert Smith, the author of "Valley of the Dee", has been a journalist all his working life. He was for more than twenty years editor of the Aberdeen "Evening Express." He writes for magazines and newspaper in this country and abroad and is the author of two books, "Grampian Ways" and "Discovering Aberdeenshire." He is a member of the Deeside Field Club and editor of its magazine, "The Deeside Field."

A set of initials that became known throughout the world began to appear on Victorian photographs in the second half of last century – G.W.W. Even after Aberdeen's pioneer photographer, George Washington Wilson, had put away his camera at the close of the century they were still to be seen. Some of these later photographs were taken by his sons, particularly Charles Wilson, who carried the Wilson name into the Edwardian age, others by company photographers. Wilson's cameras ranged all over Britain, recording everything from the grandeur of Fingal's Cave on the Isle of Staffa to the bustle of London's busy Oxford Street, where the commuters of yesteryear were photographed jostling for seats on top of horse-drawn cabs.

The Wilson collection is immense. Aberdeen University has 45,000 glass negatives of G.W.W. pictures, while a large collection is held by Aberdeen City Library. There are other collections in Aberdeen Art Gallery, in the Royal Archives at Windsor Castle, and in the Victoria and Albert Museum, the National Portrait Gallery and the British Museum.

THE ARTIST

Wilson, whose father had a croft near Banff, served his apprenticeship as a carpenter, but later trained as an artist. The step into photography was a comparatively easy one, but in his early days Wilson always described himself as "Artist and Photographer." He went to London and Paris, but in 1849 returned to Aberdeen to settle down and begin a new life. He finally turned to photography as a career in 1852.

Eighteen months later, he took his first photographs at Balmoral Castle. He became established in Aberdeen as a portrait photographer, but it was through his Royal connection (he described himself as "Photographer to the Queen" long before the title was officially bestowed) that he became more widely known. Deeside

was the cradle of his success. His camera explored well beyond the gates of Balmoral, wandering over the Deeside hills and glens, "shooting" ghillies and keepers as well as lairds and their ladies, capturing Deeside folk at work and play, and photographing towns and villages along the length of the Dee valley.

His companion on many of his photographic forays was an Aberdeen bookseller, George Walker. Walker was Boswell to Wilson's Johnson, faithfully recording their experiences in a 17-volume manuscript journal. "How well Wilson and I suited each other in these excursions," he wrote. "He was the most unselfish man I ever travelled with. He had the eye of an artist."

THE "PALACE"

In August, 1859, Wilson and Walker set out on a trip up Deeside – "to my old favourite place Braemar," said Walker. Twenty years had passed since his last visit and there were great changes. "Royalty had made Balmoral a palace," wrote Walker.

The Brig o' Bogindreep.

A.U.L. B497

"There was a railway at Banchory, the Inns had all been enlarged and become hotels, and Free Kirks had been built where some people thought 'nae kirk sud be'."

He wondered if the Braemar natives had lost their "primitive simplicity," or if a turnpike had replaced the fine walking road between Ballater and Braemar. He thought that the course of the Dee might have been changed to supply water to Balmoral and that there

would be waiters in full dress instead of comely Highland lassies who served him twenty years earlier.

The two travellers *did* find many changes, but some things remained the same. The folk of Braemar were unchanged – "They do not touch their hats when speaking to an individual with a good coat and they never vouchsafe the term 'your honour', or even the less respectful 'sir'." Walker wondered what they would have been like in another twenty years' time. He could never have foreseen that the "palace" at Balmoral would be besieged by summer tourists, that the railway would have disappeared, and that many of the kirks would have empty pews.

Now, 130 years after that 1859 visit, this book journeys up Deeside in the steps of George Washington Wilson and his literary companion. "Valley of the Dee" looks at the valley through the lens of Wilson's camera, and the pictures that he took are seen against contemporary views shot with modern SLR cameras. When G.W.W. left Aberdeen and was

"whirled away past Dr Morison's bridge and suburban Cults" his equipment was in the luggage-van – "Camera, Tent, baskets of Chemicals, Plate-boxes, and a Vasculum of two, intended for ferns, &c."

Not all the photographs in "Valley of the Dee" have the G.W.W. stamp on them. A small number were taken by two other Deeside photographers, Robert Milne and William Watson., Milne took over where Geroge Washington Wilson left off, and many

of his pictures match those of Wilson's in quality and technique. Milne, who had studios in both Aboyne and Ballater, was the "forgotten photographer" of Deeside, for he became Photographer to Her Majesty in Ballater and formed a close friendship to the Queen. Sadly, his negatives were lost; it is thought that they were destroyed in a fire in his Ballater studio.

William Watson, who came from Laurencekirk, worked in England for a time, but moved to Ballater in the late 1870s and became a professional photographer. He also took many pictures at Balmoral.

CHANGELESS

The Deeside that Wilson and Walker knew has not completely vanished; some things are changeless. As the present century moves to a close, "Valley of the Dee" looks at how things were at the end of last century. It shows how the Shakkin' Briggie looked when Wilson photographed it (and tells the story of a dream that was realised and then lost), it roars down the Feugh in the wake of the Muckle Spate, recalls the days of the loggers, putts the stone with Donald Dinnie at Potarch, and mourns a lost Chapel.

Travelling upstream, it takes G.W.W.'s camera into Balmoral and tells you about John Brown's lucky threepenny, looks at Maggie Gruer, drops down into the Colonel's Bed, and describes how a Deeside village was divided. This is Royal Deeside as it was a century ago, and as it is now, much of it still untamed, a land rich in history, stunningly beautiful, full of old tales and legends.

Bonspiels, bowlers and bools

Some things change, some things don't. The Roaring Game is still played on Deeside, but the roar has been reduced to a murmer. There are still a number of curling ponds in the valley; others have been cleaned up and put into operation again (See page 24). Todays players still wear "tammies" and "toories", but top hats and bowlers are out.

The "boolers" in the picture below were too young for bowlers; bunnets and buttoned up boots were the order of the day for them. They were concentrating on getting their marbles into the "kypie" when the picture was taken. Sadly, the great days of "dazzies" and "picks", of thumbing your bool into the kypie like the youngster below, have almost died out.

AT A CURLING BONSPIEL. 11,862. G.W.W.

A.U.L. C3989

A.C.

2

The first move to have a bridge over the River Dee at Torry came in 1871, when a plan was put forward for "a foot-bridge of wire" and payment of one halfpenny for every person who passed over it. Nothing came of the idea. In 1876, when thirty-two lives were lost in a ferry-boat disaster on the Dee, plans were drawn up for the present Victoria Bridge, which was opened in July, 1881.

When George Washington Wilson took his picture from the Torry side of the bridge, there were fishing boats drawn up on the riverbank and cows grazing in a field. When Mike Stephen took the modern picture (below) the view was totally blocked. He had to climb to the top of an oil tank to get his shot.

Lofty chimney stacks dominated Wilson's picture. Today they are all gone, but multi-storey flats mar the skyline in a different way.

UP THE DEE IN A BOATIE

Going "up the Dee in a boatie" has gone out of fashion in Aberdeen, except for Aberdeen University Boating Club teams (see below), but going up the Dee on a bike – on Riverside Drive – hasn't changed since Victorian ladies in long dresses went for a cycle run. They obviously had no traffic problems in those halycon days.

West Cults was beginning to develop as an elite suburb of Aberdeen when this photograph was taken from the south bank of the River Dee. There are more houses today – and a new reservoir – but the area still retains its air of peaceful rural tranquility, as can be seen from the picture below.

SANATORIUM, BANCHORY. 14,339. G.W.W.

A.U.L. D792

Nordrach – "Best site in Scotland"

Although this picture has the familiar G.W.W. stamp on it, it was taken by one of his sons – or a Wilson employee – seven years after his death. The caption on it reads "Sanatorium, Banchory," but early this century it was known as Nordrach – or, to give it its proper title, Nordrach-on-Dee Sanatorium. Today, people know it better as Glen o' Dee.

Nordrach was opened in 1900 as a sanatorium for tuberculosis patients. It stood in its own grounds, covering 25 acres, and it catered for thirty-six patients, although later the sanatorium was enlarged and the number was increased to seventy-five. Looking after the patients were fourteen nurses and a masseuse.

It was claimed that Deeside was " the choicest site in Scotland" for such a hospital. The bedrooms were designed in the style of "the best Continental models." The windows (as can be seen in the Wilson picture) occupied over two-thirds of the outside wall-space and were "kept open during all weathers."

The hospital authorities cashed in on the Royal presence farther up Deeside. Their brochure said that a Royal Com- mission had recommended Deeside to Queen Victoria as a Scottish health resort because of "its relative dryness, its bracing qualities, and its exceeding richness in ozone."

To these could be added its "comparatively high tempera- ture during winter months, the high percentage of sunshine which prevails (29.7), and the therapeutic vapours exhaled by its pine forests."

Aberdeen Tourist Board, please note!

The patients were able to play croquet and "modified golf," which gave them a 9-hole putting course and a 9-hole mashie course. The mashie, which is as out-of-date as the wooden driver, was the equivalent of a No. 5 iron.

Patients could also take part in minature rifle shooting, while "systematic hill climbing" was prescribed in suitable cases.

Of course, there was no National Health Service in those days; the cost of all this luxury was five guineas a week, which included personal laundry and alcohol. For those who saw themselves knocking back large whiskies while recuperating at Nordrach, it was pointed out that alcohol was "only allowed to be taken when medically pre- scribed."

Nordrach, or Glen o' Dee, has been a sanatorium, a hotel, a haven for Servicemen who con- tracted tuberculosis during the last war, and a convalescent hos- pital. It was turned into a conva- lescent hospital in 1960 when the demand for TB beds had fallen, and today it still takes convales- cent patients along with long- stay patients.

"Scotland can be proud of Glen o' Dee," said the Queen Mother – then the Queen – when she opened it to sick Service- men. Somerset Maugham was a patient at Glen o' Dee, and it was from his experiences there that he shaped the plot of his story "Sanatorium."

The distinctive design of the building came from Nodrick, in the Black Forest, and in its early days the Deeside sanatorium was called Nodrick on Dee. Some of the timber for the build- ing of the hospital came from the Black Forest.

Not much has changed since the Wilson photograph was taken, although the building has begun to show its years. The two birch trees on left of the picture are fully grown, but the others have vanished.

"THE SHAKIN' BRIGGIE", CULTS. 14,682. G.W.W.

Plea for the Shakkin' Brig

From the Evening Express, 1st April, 1921.

Come a' my frien's an' list tae me
A kin'ly ear len' tae my plea
A helpin' han', oh, may ye gie
    As frien' tae frien'
Tae set me siccer ower the Dee
    That rins atween.

For mony a 'ear I laught tae scorn
The wimplin' stream at nicht or morn,
An' thocht the day wad ne'er be born
    Tae change my state,
But, haith, my foun's been fairly torn
    Wi' yon wild spate.

The tumlin' waters reeve an' tore
At my stoot biggins, back and fore
They steid as they had steid afore
    But waes me noo,
They're frail an' shakk'n' tae the core,
    An' crackit thro'.

I fear the blusterin' winter's blast
I fear the swirling waters vast,
As madly, seaward, rushin' past
    They buffet sair
I mayna hae the pith at last
    Tae thole them mair.

Oh, ye who trod my slender pile
An' hained thy shanks fu' mony a mile,
Or, wooed by Dee's sweet sil'vry wile,
    Roamed o'er my banks,
Turn kin'ly thochts tae me a fyle,
    An' show they thanks.

An' ye fond lovers, maid an' wicht
Wha sought my path in sweet meenlicht,
Or trystit aft on mirkest nicht
    At my wide span,
Gin ye wad wish tae see me richt,
    Pit thee thy han'.

Ye lichtsome-hertit, happy throng,
Wha' aft, wi' mirth an' merry song,
Hae spent the simmer's day sae long
    Aroon my feet,
I pray thy help tae mak' me strong
    Aul' time tae meet.

Oh, hearken, then, my earnest plea,
Leal lovers o' the winding Dee,
Haud oot a han' tae succour me
    In time o' need,
An' a' my days prood thanks I'll gie
    For thy kind deed.

G.P.D.
Stoneywood

"We wid hae been furl't doon tae Aiberdeen"

The Shakkin' Briggie today.

Mike Stephen

From the window of his manse at Banchory-Devenick, the Rev. Dr. George Morison watched members of his congregation cross the bridge over the River Dee and make their way along the embankment to his church. It was a dream that he had nursed for over fifty years – to see a bridge that would allow people on the north side of the Dee to get to kirk even if the river was too rough to cross by boat. Now his dream had come true – the Shakkin' Briggie had been built.

When it was opened, Dr. Morison reminded his congregation that they no longer had a reason for non-attendance. The excuse, he said, had always been, "We wid hae been furl't doon tae Aiberdeen, if nae droon't, gin we'd tried rowin' ower the water on Sunday."

WEALTHY MINISTER

The new suspension bridge was known as St. Devenick's Bridge when it was built in 1837. Later, in recognition of the fact that the money for it had come out of the minister's own pocket (it cost £1400), it was called Morison's Bridge. Even so, not everyone was pleased. Some farmers said sneeringly, "Foo didna the wealthy minister mak' his briggie tae tak' carts ower't?"

To generations of Cults folk, as well as to Aberdonians, it has always been the Shakkin' Briggie. Today, it is still shakkin', but only just. Its rusty skeleton reaches out over the River Dee at Cults as if making a last desperate attempt to regain its former glory. Half-way across it gives up, dropping its dreams into the turbulent water below.

Looking at George Washington Wilson's picture of the Shakkin' Briggie it is hard to understand why it was allowed

to become the broken clutter of scrap iron that it is now, for it was a lovely bridge. They certainly thought so when they built it 150 years ago. In 1840, they celebrated with a big public dinner in a marquee on the north side of the Dee, close to the bridge. It was a "Thank you" to Dr. Morison.

Floods were the biggest threat to the Shakkin' Briggie, as they were to other bridges in the Dee Valley. In August, 1914, the embankment path along the south side of the river, between the bridge and the South Deeside Road, was practically destroyed, and in the spate of October, 1920, the south end of the bridge was badly damaged. The bridge was kept open, but people had to pick their way over the wreckage.

The *Aberdeen Daily Journal* opened a special fund for its repair and a Doric poem signed "G.P.D." (G.P. Dunbar, Stoneywood) made a plea for "a helpin' han'." The public responded with £500 and two years later a crowd of 100 turned up for the re-opening cermony. Ominously, it was carried out in pouring rain.

After that, it was downhill – or downriver – all the way. In 1957 an appeal for £5000 raised only £400. The following year the district council gave up responsibility for repairs and by 1966 the damage done by storm, floods and erosion had raised the bill to £27,000. No one wanted to know about the poor old Shakkin' Briggie. For local councils it

was a bridge too far – they even put up barbed wire to stop people crossing. Meanwhile, the south side slowly collapsed.

Councillor Gordon Adams, of Aberdeen District Council, who had been on a working party studying the feasibility of restoring the bridge, said bluntly that there was no money.

"The best solution would be to dismantle the damned thing and build it somewhere else," he declared, "If they can sell London Bridge to the Americans, surely we can find a home for the Shakkin' Briggie."

NO HAPPY THRONG

Sadly, nothing came of the idea. Today there is no "lichtsome-hertit, happy throng" willing to cough up £500, far less £5000 or more, to help save the Shakkin' Briggie. Nothing goes under it except ducks, nothing goes over it except the nostalgic glances of folk who are old enough to remember when they played "wi' mirth and merry song" around its feet.

One idea put forward in 1968 was that the Shakkin' Briggie should be moved upstream to become a walk-over bridge for the Brig o' Feugh. Nothing ever came of that either. It would have been a happy solution for the St. Devenick's Bridge, for the Brig o' Feugh has itself withstood years of battering from sudden spates.

Hedged in at Crathes

Crathes Castle, which was one of the first North-east castles to be opened to the public by the National Trust for Scotland, has more than its Great Hall and its famous painted ceilings to interest visitors. It also has its huge Irish yew hedges.

The yew hedges, which date from 1702, enclose a series of small gardens. In the contemporary picture on left the castle is framed by two of the hedges, while George Washington Wilson's picture below shows the grounds as they were a century ago.

On the opposite page is Wilson's picture of the magnificent dining hall at Crathes, while the lower picture shows another well-known Deeside castle – Drum. It was built in the late 13th century to keep guard over the Royal Forest of Drum.

The castle and its policies were handed over to the National Trust in 1976 under the will of the 24th laird, H.Q. Forbes Irvine.

R.S.

CRATHES CASTLE. 309. G.W.W.

A.U.L. C1035

9

CRATHES CASTLE, DINING HALL. 2767. G.W.W.

DRUM CASTLE FROM THE NORTH.

A.U.L. E2273

A.U.L. C401

10

A.U.L. A2I69

Mike Stephen

Inchmarlo House

Inchmarlo House, near Banchory, is a gracious Georgian mansion which has been converted into a continuing care community – a new concept in providing for the retirement needs of the over 55's.

It is both a retirement home and a nursing home, and there are sheltered apartments and houses for those who prefer their own accommodation.

The setting is Queen Victoria Park, its name a reminder that Queen Victoria was so captivated by Inchmarlo that she ordered her coach to be driven through the estate on her way to Balmoral.

George Washington Wilson's photograph captures Inchmarlo's beauty and serenity. The lower picture shows a group of residents at the home.

F. FEUGH. BANCHORY-TERNAN. 10,326   G.W.W.

The Feugh cam' rairin doon fae Birse,
  An' swept the haughs o' Stra'an,
Horse, pigs, an' kye were droont i' Dye,
  An' sheep by scores in A'an.

A cadger body, Johnny Joss,
  Nae far fae Bogendreep,
Lost shaltie, cairtie, creels an' a'
  At ae unlucky sweep.

– SEE PAGES 13 and 14 –

Top – the Brig o' Feugh.
Bottom – the Brig o' Bogindreep.

THE MUCKLE SPATE

"The Feugh cam' rairin' doon fae Birse an' swept the haughs o' Stra'an . . ." So wrote David Grant in his classic "Muckle Spate of 'Twenty-nine," an epic poem describing what happened when Deeside was caught up in the disastrous floods of 1829. During that watery holocaust the River Dee rose to 27ft. above its normal level at Banchory. Haystacks, cattle, pigs, sheep and poultry, as well as trees and household goods, were swept downstream and came bobbing up in the waters of Aberdeen harbour.

Sir Thomas Dick Lauder, in *The Moray Floods*, described it as "this awful admonition to a sinful land." Deeside must have sinned more than other parts of the country, for it frequently suffered from severe flooding in the 18th and 19th centuries – in 1799, when the first bridge at Ballater was swept away; in 1812, when the Bridge of Potarch was damaged; in 1827, when a spate overturned the ferry at Aboyne; and during the Muckle Spate of 1829.

Three bridges south of Banchory were pounded by the Muckle Spate – the Brig o' Feugh, on the outskirts of the town, and the Brigs of Bogendreep and Dye, both spanning the Water of Dye,

The private bridge at Feugh Lodge, upstream from the Brig o' Feugh.

which joins the Feugh at Strachan. The high humped-back Brig of Dye, the oldest bridge in the Dee Valley, was built for travellers going over the Cairn-Mounth. Up till then they had crossed the stream at the Ford of Dye. After the bridge was built many people were unwilling to pay the toll and crossed the ford.

The Dye was a treacher-ous river – "one of the most impetuous waters within the Kingdom, where many have perished," said a report in 1681. The bridge was needed because of the "great and sudden Innunda-tions," but it was in danger of being "spoyled by storms." David Grant's poem said that in the Muckle Spate "horses, pigs, an' kye were droont i' Dye." The Brig o' Bogendreep wasn't much better –

A cadger body, Johnnie Joss,
Nae far fae Bogendreep,
Lost shawltie, cairtie, creels an' a'
At ae unlucky sweep.

The Brig o' Feugh was built about 1790 to take traffic from the Slug road. It is a romantic little spot. A small car park was built near it so that motorists could stop and watch salmon leaping in the Feugh. Upstream, a private bridge which George Washington Wilson photographed crosses the Water of Feugh at Feugh Lodge.

David Grant, the son of a local farmer, was six years old when the Muckle Spate unleashed its anger on Deeside. It is thought that he wrote his poem some twenty years later. The events of that August day in 1829 are vividly and hilariously recorded in the poem, which relates how the dyster (dyer), "like a drookit rat," escaped from Dalsack, how Fytie (the farmer at Whitestone) woke to find that the fusky-pig (whisky jar) had gone, and how the souter (shoemaker) at Dalbreck lost "a dizzen harn sacks (linen shirts)."

Excerpts from the "Muckle Spate" are given on Page 14. They are well worth reading, for, as our Feughside poet told us, there has never been "anither spate like auchteen twenty-nine."

The Brig o' Dye as G.W.W. saw it.

Just like Noah's Flood

Tho' I was only but a bairn
    In auchteen twenty-nine,
The mem'ry o' the Muckle Spate
    Has never left my min'.

We had a byous weety time,
    A week, or maybe mair,
The eident rain kept pelting on,
    Nae single hoor was fair.

An' then for four-an'-twenty hoors
    There followed a doonfa'
The like o' which, sin' Noah's flood,
    The warl' never saw.

The thunner rum'lt roon the hills,
    The howes were in a soom,
We thocht the warl', owergaen wi' age,
    Drew near the crack o' doom.

Store-house at Mar Lodge ruined.

The feugh cam' rairin' doon fae Birse,
    An' swept the haughs o' Stra'an;
Horse, pigs, an' kye were droont i' Dye,
    An' sheep by scores in A'an.

An' yarn reels, an' spinnin' wheels,
    An' bowie, cogs, and caups,
An' tables, chairs, an' cutty steels,
    On ane anither's taps.

An' girnels, aumries, washin' tubs,
    An' smuggled whisky kegs,
Cheese chessils, butter kits, an' kirns,
    An' couple bauks an' legs.

An' skeps o' bees, an' sowen sieves,
    An' skulls, an' tattie creels,
An' reets, an' trunks, an' taps o' trees,
    An' palin' bars, an' deals.

At Ennochie a cluckin' hen
    Wis sittin' in a kist,
Baith it an' her were sweelt awa'
    Afore the creatur' wist;

We saw her passin' near Heugh-head
    As canty as ye like,
Afore her ark a droonit stirk,
    Ahint a droonit tyke.

We left her near the Burn o' Frusk,
    An' speculatit lang
Gin she were carri't to the sea
    Afore her ark gaed wrang.

An' may be spairt by Davie Jones
    To bring her cleckin' oot,
Gin she wad rear them like a hen
    Or like a water coot?

A smachet o' a lassie serv't
    The souter at Dalbreck,
He lost a dizzen harn sacks
    Through her entire neglec'.

She left them bleachin' o' the green,
    Wi' ither claes a curn;
The spate cam' on upo' the nicht,
    An' a' gaed doon the burn.

Bridge of Ballater wrecked.

He took the smatchet wi' his nieve
    A riesle on the lug,
'Tak' that,' quo' he, 'ye careless shard,
    'I's gar ye wear my marks.'

'I'll tell my mither noo,' she cried,
    'As sure as I'm alive,
She'll gar the souter smairt afore
    The lawwers o' Stanehive.'

Aul' Willie Wilson lost his coo,
    An' never got anither,
He left her near the waterside
    a' nicht upo' the tether.

She brak' the tether in a fleg,
    An' clam upon a heugh,
But mist a fit, or took a dwam,
    An' tum'lt i' the Feugh.

She sank into the muckle pot,
    Aneth the kelpie's stane,
An' afterwards wis swirl't awa',
    He lost her skin an' bane.

Peer Tam M'Rory's breeding soo,
    Gaed doon the Burn o' Cammie,
A muckle loss, an' sair heart-brak'
    Baith to the wife an' Tammie.

For they were just expectin' pigs,
    An' pigs were gey an' dear,
The litter wad a' paid the rent,
    An' left a note, or near.

My sister lost a brocket lam'
    She got fae Tammie Durrit –
'wis said she micht 'a got a croon
O gweed fyte siller fot it.

Peer silly ted, it brak' its string
    An' ran upo' the brae,
An' saw a sheep come bleatin' doon
    Upon a coll o' hay.

We didna ken – it micht a' thocht
    The bleatin' sheep its mither,
At onyrate it jumpit in,
    An' baith were droon't thegither.

But wae's my hairt for aul' Meg Mill,
    Far kent as 'Birlin' Meg,'
Fae Persie to the mou' o' Feugh
    Nane got a gryter fleg.

Out-house at Mar Lodge ruined.

'Noo, faur ye gyaun?' quo' Cammie's herd;
    Quo' Meg, 'To Clochnaben,
Rin, laddie, rin, an' leave yer beasts,
    The world's at an en'!

Rin, laddie, rin, an' dinna stan'
    An' stare as ye were wud,
For Gweed forgie's, the sins o' men
    Hiv brocht a second flood.

Rin, laddie, rin to Clochnaben,
    There's nae a glint tae spare,
The angels micht rax doon for us
    Gin we cud but get there.'

SLUG OF DESS. 14,407 G.W.W.

This picturesque little waterfall is the Slug of Dess, tucked away in a wooded ravine not far from the North Deeside Road, west of Kincardine O'Neil. There are various forms of "Slug" – Slock, Sloch or Sloc. The name means "burn of the big gully."

15

A brace of hotels

These two Deeside hotels have been relatively untouched by the passage of time. Both show exteriors that are virtually unchanged since George Washington Wilson photographed them. The Learney Arms Hotel in Torphins still has its dyke, but the trees on the pavement have gone. The Tor-na-Coille Hotel in Banchory still has its elegant balcony.

High Street, Banchory-Ternan, looking W. 10.331. G.W.W.

A.U.L. A2726

Spot the difference

There are no prizes for spotting the difference between these two pictures. Traffic, for one thing . . . . any motorist who has tried to park his car on Banchory's High Street must look at George Washington Wilson's photograph and sigh for the days of the horse and buggy.

Some things haven't changed. The chemists shop is still there, with the same mortar and pestle above the door. Note the smaller sign on the nearby wall lamp, which has the words "Post Office" written on the glass.

Three street lamps mark the length of the High Street. They may not have been as tall as their modern counterparts, but they had a lot more character.

I wonder what the boy in the knickerbockers was thinking as he stood watching Aberdeen's pioneer photographer at work?

Mike Stephen

The girl who saw G.W.W. at work . . .

Like the boy in knickerboker trousers (see opposite page) the wee girl in the picture was obviously fascinated when she saw G.W.W. at work.

Who was she? Did she ever see the photograph when she grew up — or show it to her grandchildren? Does her family still live in Banchory?

Perhaps she appeared for one brief moment in front of Wilson's lens and then disappeared for all time. Whoever she was, Wilson was probably delighted to see her there, for he liked to have people in his pictures.

The photograph shows the Burnett Arms Hotel and the old Free Church. The changes that have taken place since Wilson photographed this corner of Banchory can be seen in the picture on the right.

Mike Stephen

FREE CHURCH AND BURNETT ARMS HOTEL, BANCHORY. 10,333. G.W.W.

A.U.L. C5719

18

GOLF COURSE, BANCHORY, TAKING IN ROE'S POT NEAR INCHMARLO. 14885. G.W.W.

From Bogeys to Buggies

When they took to the fairways of Banchory golf course in the good old days they were properly dressed . . . . jackets, collars, ties, even felt hats.

The picture above shows what the well-dressed golfer was wearing a century ago. It was taken by Washington Wilson at Roe's Pot, near Inchmarlo.

The scenery may not have changed, but the clothes have – and the transport! They knew about bogeys in the old days, but not about buggies. The chap playing his stroke in G.W.W.'s picture would have "duffed" his chip shot if he had seen that come bumping up the fairway.

Banchory golfers who look at this picture will never again complain about the state of the fairways . . . or the greens. The caddy on the right is more interested in G.W.W.'s camera than he is in the player's putt. In the corner (top right) is the Bridge of Dee, seen at closer range in the tee shot picture taken by Mike Stephen.

Top — Potarch Bridge is the setting for this idyllic scene on Deeside on a summer's day a century ago. The name Potarch comes from poll tairbh, meaning the bull's pool, a pool in the Dee here. Below — Two guests at the Potarch Hotel try to lift the Dinnie stones, which the great athlete Donald Dinnie carried over the bridge. See story and picture on opposite page.

DONALD DINNIE – GIANT OF THE DEE

A short distance upstream from the spot where George Washington Wilson took his tranquil picture of the River Dee at Potarch is Jock Young's Loup. The Loup, or Leap, is a jagged outcrop of rock which got its name when Jock, a notorious tinker, made a spectacular escape from his guards while being taken from Aboyne to Aberdeen after being arrested for killing another gypsy. He broke away from his captors, raced to the river bank, and with one enormous "loup" sailed through the air to the other side. He was eventually captured and executed at Aberdeen in 1801.

Jock Young came from a notorious family of "cairds" or tinkers. He is said to have broken out of half the prisons in Scotland. It was either Jock or his elder brother, Peter, who during an escape from Aberdeen prison, let all the other prisoners out and wrote on the door, "Rooms to let·"

The legendary loup over the Dee was made before Potarch Bridge was built. After the bridge was erected, Potarch became known for another athletic feat. It was there that the famous "heavy" athlete, Donald Dinnie, crossed the bridge carrying two stones that were said to be impossible to lift.

The Dinnie Stones now lie outside the door of Potarch Hotel, challenging visitors to raise them. Plenty people have tried; no one has succeeded. The stones were, in fact, Donald's practice weights, and over the years they have acquired an almost mythical reputation.

Donald, who was born at Aboyne in 1837 and died in 1916, was the son of Robert Dinnie, a mason and writer. He was the eldest of six brothers. His fame spread far beyond Deeside, for he competed all over the world, in America, Australia, New Zealand and South Africa.

He is said to have won 10,000 prizes, including 150 championships, and to have earned over £26,000 in prize money — a small fortune in those days. The picture above shows him with so many medals on his chest that only a "heavy" could have worn them without being bent over.

He was certainly a mighty man. He was 6ft. in height, with a chest of 48in. a thigh of 26½in, and a calf of 17¼in. During training his weight was 15st.

Donald kept a hotel at Kincardine O'Neil for three years and later took over the Kintore Arms Hotel at Auchenblae. Now, more than seventy years after his death, the Din-

Donald Dinnie and his medals.

nie name is once again linked with the hotel business, drawing visitors to the hotel where he practised tossing the caber and putting the stone.

Stewart Spence, the well-known Aberdeen hotelier, has taken over Potarch Hotel in partnership with Michael and Linda Boyle and is developing the Dinnie theme.

The folk idling by the Dee in Washington Wilson's picture, the girls in their boaters, the men in their bowlers, may have seen Donald with his weights, but here they are more interested in enjoying the sunshine and watching the river slip by. It must have been a dry summer, for the water level is low.

It wasn't always so dry in this corner of Deeside. Potarch was where the Cairn o' Mount road crossed the Dee by a ford at Inchbare, a little below the bridge, and the crossing was often made difficult by floods and ice. Between 1698 and 1706 a collection was made in church to assist in "building a bridge over Dee at Pittarch," but it was 1812 before a bridge was built. When it was nearly completed it was almost demolished by loose logs being floated down the river.

The inn was erected in the same year as the bridge and at one time there was a market there. Now, like their Victorian forbears, picnickers sit by the river bank or play on the Green opposite the hotel.

Halt for the roaring game!

The curling stop at the Loch of Aboyne.

Mike Stephen

The picture by George Washington Wilson shows the old Deeside railway line running into Aboyne, but there was a stop before the trains reached the station — a curling stop. The platform can still be seen on the edge of the Loch of Aboyne. Curlers stepped down from the train on to the ice.

Bunnets and bowlers were worn (see opposite page), with the occasional top-hat and a scattering of tammies and toories. In Wilson's picture, a few ladies can be seen hovering in the background, but the men were more interested in sweeping the ice than sweeping them off their feet.

There is still a Deeside Curling Association. Bonspiels are played on ponds like Logie-Coldstone, and in the past few years the Roaring Game has made something of a comeback. There is a curling pond on the Royal estate at Easter Balmoral, used in summer as a tennis court.

AT A CURLING BONSPIEL.   11,043.   G.W.W.

Bowler-hatted curlers sweeping the ice on the loch.

24

In the Land of the Lochs

A.U.L. C7740

The old Aboyne — and the new — are seen in the photographs in these two pages. The picture by Washington Wilson above shows the Station Square a century ago, empty of traffic, sleeping in the sun. A group of boys lounge at the entrance to the station. Perhaps it was this kind of scene that made Wilson's companion, George Walker, say that Aboyne had once been "a dull, half-way house." "The Railway Terminus and approach here," he wrote, "wants the beauty of that at Banchory, but carried as the line is, through a part of the Loch, the traveller will still be reminded that he is in the Land of Lochs." More than a hundred years later the Railway Terminus has gone — and Aboyne's Station Square (see below) is busier than it has ever been.

Mike Stephen

George Walker thought that Aboyne was "passed and speedily forgotten" until it got its hotel — the Huntly Arms, seen in Wilson's picture above. Walker said that Aboyne was "beautified by its large, handsome hotel, with 'classical' waiters in lace neckties." Crowds gathered outside the hotel to see the coach arriving. "Sportsmen, with gay knickerbockers of a loud pattern, are starting for the moors," he wrote. "Handsome carriages are arriving or departing, and fashion rules the day." Aboyne, declared Walker, had become a "lodging-house village." It is still a lodging-house village today, as well as a commuter town, but the coaches and carriages have been replaced by cars and bikes, as our picture below shows.

DOWN THE DEE ON LOGS
– how Frank won a £50 bet

Frank Harper on the last lap of his journey by log raft.

Back in 1930 a young Aberdeen University student took a trip down the River Dee on a raft of logs to raise money for charity. It was said that in the old days forestry students spent their summer vacations rafting logs down the Dee, but logging had died out by the turn of the century. Now, a £50 cheque for Aberdeen Charities Week awaited the student who showed that it could still be done.

Frank Harper, a forestry student from Aboyne, took up the challenge. He started below Banchory and, according to a report in the *Evening Express*, "went down the river at a spanking pace." It was thought that he might have difficulty passing under the Bridge of Dee, but, keeping to the south bank, "guiding his raft like a Venetian gondolier," he swept under the far arch at a tremendous speed and pulled into the bank.

His biggest problem was in slowing himself down so that his arrival at Victoria Bridge coincided with the appearance of Lord Provost Rust. The Lord Provost was there to shake his hand, congratulate him on his courage and endurance, and hand over a cheque for £50.

Done at "spanking pace"

Frank, now retired from his post as a head forestry officer in the Gold Coast (Ghana), looks down on the tumbling waters of the Dee from his home in Aboyne and remembers his river journey. For two brief hours on that day in 1930 he revived a tradition stretching back through the eighteenth and nineteenth centuries, when timber floating was in full swing on the Dee.

He has a copy of a lithograph, dated about 1860, showing the old suspension bridge at Aboyne. Underneath it a lone logger is punting a raft in the way that he himself did as a student. He also has a lithograph showing a kilted lumberman on a log raft under the Shakkin' Briggie. It was drawn by Eliza Mearns, a niece of Dr George Morison, who built the bridge.

The exploitation of North-east forests for use outside the area began about 1600. Up till then, because of their inaccessibility, they met only local needs, but log floating as a method of extracting timber began in the 18th century.

The loggers of Deeside have never been given the recognition they deserve. They had a tough, dangerous, job. The logs were tied together with ropes, rings and "dogs" (mechanical grips), and the loggers, or floaters, used guiding ropes and poles to float the rafts down-river. They were always wet.

The American system of loose logging was rarely used, because logs piling up against the piers of bridges could seriously damage them. The building of Potarch Bridge in 1812 was held up when single trees, left on the river bank for "flooding," were swept against the half-built bridge, nearly destroying it. The bridge was completed in June, 1814.

Timber was floated down the River Dee to Aberdeen from as far away as Glen Derry. A notorious Deeside poacher, Alexander Davidson, became a timber merchant for a

(cont. on next page)

The old suspension bridge at Aboyne as seen in Wilson's picture and (above) an old lithograph.

time, buying a large quantity of wood in Glen Derry from the Earl of Fife. About 1820 he built a large dam on the Derry so that he could get enough water to float the logs down the Dee. A big jam of logs was called a "cairn," and floaters trying to free them with crowbars often found the whole mass breaking loose under their feet. Many were crushed to death trying to break up a "cairn."

An incident with a "cairn" at Invercauld landed Sandy Davidson in trouble. In the River Dee opposite Invercauld House there was a huge stone which often obstructed floats of timber. The floaters decided to blast it, but the Invercauld factor took out a court interdict to stop them. Defying the interdict, the loggers set out to blow up the stone, but the factor gathered some men together to stop them.

A temporary gangway of logs had been laid from the bank to the cairn. When the factor stepped on to it, some of the floaters loosened its moorings in the hope that he would be carried away. Davidson rushed on to the gangway, grabbed the factor in his arms, and carried him back to the bank. The next minute the gangway was swept down the river.

Davidson got no thanks from the factor.

Frank on his raft.

He carried on with his logging, but he found that the cost of floating timber seventy miles down the Derry and Dee to Aberdeen was excessive. After he had lost money in his timber dealings he went back to poaching.

In 1881, James Allan, who kept a "Lumberman's Log," worked for a time at Blackhall, Banchory, dragging timber from the high land west of Scolty and Blackhall to the river bank opposite Cairnton, where the logs were floated down the Dee to a timber mill at Silverbank. The timber mill is still there to-day, on the outskirts of Banchory.

"We had a day of ten hours," he wrote, "and were glad if we could complete six

drags of one half or three-quarters of a mile to the river bank. He thought that these were the last trees to be formed into rafts and systematically floated down the Dee. "I never heard of floating after that," he said.

The most dangerous part of the Dee for the floaters was the Glisters, opposite Invercannie Waterworks, on Blackhall water. Here, rocks in the bed of the river were blasted to make an easier passage for rafts. It was said that at Blackhall the river rose and fell in good weather even when there was no rain.

The loggers worked hard and played hard. There were a number of "river-inns" where they could pull in to eat — and drink. Their favourite game was Bawbee Nap. One of these river-inns was Cutaway Cottage at Cambus-o'-May. When the railway came, ending the need for floating timber, a corner of the building was sliced off to let the line pass on its way to Ballater.

There was also a river inn at the ford from Drumoak to Durris, opposite Dalmaik farm. The hostess there was Meggie Davidson, sister of the poacher Sandy Davidson. When the railway came and the floaters disappeared, Meggie went about the district with a pair of baskets on her arms collecting eggs.

The modern bridge and Frank Harper's cottage.

"It had an awfu' shak' on it . . ."

There have been three suspension bridges over the River Dee at Aboyne. The first was built in 1828 after a woman and daughter were drowned when the Bontie ferry overturned in a spate. The scaffolding was still on the new bridge when it was swept away in the floods of 1829.

A second bridge was erected in 1831. It was a narrow, graceful structure that had a "Shakkin' Briggie" look about it – and, according to one report, it was "noted for oscillation·" A resident of the time put it in more down-to-earth language – "It was awfu' slim an' had an awfu' shak' on it."

By the time the 1860s had come around it had deteriorated so much that it was shut down and the ferry brought back into use. The third suspension bridge was completed in 1871.

The bridge in our picture has gone, but one thing remains. The distinctive cottage at the north end of the bridge is still there, although it, too, has seen changes over the years.

Frank Harper, the floater of the £50 cheque challenge in 1930, lives in Bridgend Cottage. Ask him how old he is and he is liable to point to a monkey puzzle tree in his garden. It was planted the year he was born – 1910. He remembers seeing the third suspension bridge when he was a child.

His father, James Harper, who owned William Brown, the fishing tackle shop in

Frank outside Bridgend Cottage, with the monkey puzzle tree on the right.

Aberdeen, bought Bridgend in the 1920s, and leased it before that. The house is really a three-in-one structure. There was originally a croft there, and part of it survives in one side of the house. It was retained when the Marquis of Huntly built the present cottage.

The back of the house has an extension made from local granite. They were used when W. Cunliffe Brooks, the Laird of Glentanar, took over Bridgend. He opened a number of quarries on his estate to try to relieve unemployment.

Frank regards the cottage as "a bit of a folly" because of its Palladian look. There is no doubt that it has a certain pseudo-classical appearance, but it also has character. Across the road is the Boat Inn. It was sometimes known as Bridgend Inn, and in its original form was one long thatched house.

The ford was a few hundred yards east of where the bridge is now, and the Bontie (or Bowntie) ferry was farther up-river. John Ross, a ferryman at Waterside of Birse, nearly opposite Aboyne, is said to have featured in a Jacobite song, although some people are sceptical about the story. It went –

I'll gie John Ross anither bawbee
To ferry me o'er to Charlie;
We'll o'er the water, we'll o'er the sea,
We'll o'er the water to Charlie

There are two large stone pillars at each end of Frank Harper's front garden. These, and a third pillar on the opposite side of the road, carried lights for the bridge. One of the pillars can be seen in the photograph. A lot of water has passed under the Bontie bridge since oil lamps lit the way for travellers crossing the Dee on their way south.

A magnificent view of Glentanar House, taken by Washington Wilson last century.

The old mansion house of Glentanar, which once stood in the heart of one of Deeside's loveliest glens.

● Glentanar House was built by Sir William Cunliffe Brooks when he purchased the estate in 1890. He also acquired the estates of Ferrar and Aboyne Castle. The estate was bought by George Coats, of the sewing-cotton firm of Paisley, who was created the 1st Baron Glentanar in 1916. He died in 1918 and was succeded by his son, Thomas Coats.

The lower picture shows the rear of the present building, with the ballroom on the right.

Braeloine Bridge

Hundreds of visitors use the old, hump-backed Braeloine Bridge, which crosses the Water of Tanar near the public car park and visitor's centre. It takes them to the Chapel of St. Lesmo (opposite page) along the old road to the south. There is, appropriately, a water trough near the bridge with the Gaelic inscription, "A Hundred Thousand Welcomes."

Below is Wilson's picture of an old cottage near the Fungle at Parkside. The village can be seen in the distance across the Dee.

Mike Stephen

COTTAGE AT ABOYNE. 10,148. G.W.W.

A.U.L. A789

The Chapel of St. Lesmo.

R.S.

Anyone for tennis?

The Laird of Glentanar, Sir William Cunliffe Brooks, with his wife and a party of house guests outside Glentanar House. The ladies were obviously ready for the tennis court. The gentlemen, as the antlers indicate, went in for more violent sports.

The Laird's deadly "snake"

The name Wilcebe Road isn't in any street directory. It can be seen on a back road on Belrorie Hill on the Glentanar estate. The explanation for the name comes when you think of Wilcebe . . . Will C.B. . . . William Cunliffe Brooks.

Sir William Cunliffe Brooks was an eccentric laird of Glentanar who stamped his initials "WCB" on stones, wells and monuments all over the estate. He took it a step further when he put up a permanent memorial to himself in the shape of a road sign.

Today, Glen Tanar is owned by the Hon. Jean Bruce, granddaughter of George Coats, the first Baron of Glentanar, who bought it after Cunliffe Brooks's death in 1900.

The estate was opened up to the public a number of years ago through the Glen Tanar Charitable Trust and part of it is a national nature reserve. Cunliffe Brooks's influence is everywhere . . . on the distinctive buildings, in the lovely Chapel of St. Lesmo, in the estate offices and school, and in the inscriptions scattered about Glen Tanar.

"WCB" had a passion for inscriptions. They are cut out on stones throughout the estate, particularly on the wells in Glentanar. One well near Wilcebe Road has the warning, "The worm of the still is the deadliest snake of the Hill" – a reminder that illicit whisky-making was once rife in the glen.

There are six wells spaced out along Wilcebe Road, including one with the inscription, "Well to know when you are well off." There is another which says "Drink, Thank, Think."

The biggest well is on the South Deeside Road, at the old glen Tanar school, built to commemorate Queen Victoria's diamond jubilee. There is an ugly uncut stone in place of one of the blocks of dressed granite. This was Sir William's way of illustrating what happened when you got a square peg in a round hole.

The Laird of Glentanar, Sir William Cunliffe Brooks (against tree) with a house party at Glentanar. Both ladies and gentlemen sport fancy hats, but the prize for novelty goes to the gent with the fancy walking stick.

34

House Parties

No Deeside estate was without its house party in Victorian times . . . and the same applies today. Here (top picture), Sir William Cunliffe-Brooks, seen with his dog in his lap, entertains guests at Glentanar. The group below, which includes Madama Tosti, was photographed at Glenmuick House.

When some guests acted the goat!

The children of house guests on Deeside often had nannies, but not many had nanny goats. These youngsters in a house party at Invercauld House found themselves with a miniature carriage driven by goat-power. The picture was taken in October 1900. The excitement clearly went to the ladies' heads. Their millinery creations were striking, but three of them decided to copy the gentlemen and go for bonnets. First prize in the millinery stakes, however went to the children – and the goats!

A.C.

The spectacular rocky bowl known as the Burn o' Vat lies at the foot of Culblean hill, looking out over the twin lochs of Kinord and Davan. The name is a direct translation of the Gaelic, burn of the dabhach. the tub or vat. It was once thought to be the hiding place of Rob Roy MacGregor, but, in fact, it was another well-known outlaw, Gilderoy, who used it. The recess where he sheltered is masked by a miniture waterfall (not shown in Wilson's picture), big enough to hold one man.

This was how Loch Kinord at Dinnet was seen in Washington Wilson's time – and on left as it is today. The cottage is now a Nature Conservancy visitors' centre. The wide-open view has gone. The whole area is covered in moorland and closed in by trees and shrubs, with picnic spots laid along the road to Tarland. A lone traveller on a horse and trap can be seen on the road – today cars and holidaymakers pass along it.

Know this bridge?

There have been some thirty bridges over the River Dee in the past two centuries. Some have been demolished, others have been rebuilt. How many people recognise this one? It is, in fact, the original iron girder bridge at Dinnet, built in 1861-62 to replace a ford and ferry there.

It should have been completed in 1861, but on the day that it was expected to be finished one of the girders fell into the river. It was completed in the summer of 1862.

The folk in that part of Deeside had a brand new bridge, but what they didn't have was a decent road at either end of it. The cart track that passed for a road was so bad that if, for example, a funeral had to go from Glentanar, on the south side of the River Dee, to Coldstone on the north side it had to go round by Aboyne and avoid the Dinnet bridge.

It wasn't until the railway was extended to Ballater and a new station built at Dinnet that a proper road was constructed.

The iron girder bridge was rebuilt in 1935.

The old ruined Kirk of Tullich is all that is left of a hamlet that once had a market, a post office and an inn known as the Change-house at the Stile of Tullich.

The kirk, which dates from about 1400, was built on the site of St. Nathalan's Chapel.

In Wilson's picture there are only a scattering of tombstones, whereas today's photograph shows that the burial ground now extends outside the wall of the kirkyard. The trees inside the ruin have gone.

Tullich faded away when Pannanich, across the Dee, became famous for its "miracle" wells. The ferry which took people across the river to Pannanich was unable to cope. A new bridge was built farther upstream – and Ballater began to grow.

When I roved a young Highlander
o'er the dark heath
And climbed thy steep summit
O, Morven of snow.

Byron "widna tak' a tellin'"

The farm of Ballaterach can be reached by a track branching off the South Deeside Road some three miles east of Ballater. It sits on the edge of moorland stretching away to Pannanich and over the Black Moss to Etnach and Mount Keen. Here, nearly two centuries ago, the "illtricket nickum, Geordie Byron," spent his holidays fishing, bathing in the river, and falling in love with the Deeside hills.

He also, according to some reports, fell in love with the Ballaterach farmer's daughter, a romantic idea fuelled in writers' minds by the poet's lines on "my sweet Mary." Time and commonsense has withered this grand passion, for Byron was a little lame boy of eight when he was at Ballaterach and the girl, Mary Robertson, was not much older. She died in 1867 at the age of 82, which would have made her eleven at the time.

Yet he was obviously attracted to her. He often talked about her to a lad called Stewart Clark, who went fishing with him at Gairnshiel. There are contradictory descriptions of "Sweet Mary." She was described as "very pretty, with long flowing ringlets of gold," but she was also said to be the plainest of the two Robertson sisters.

There is another school of thought which says that "sweet Mary" was actually Mary Duff, a cousin, who played with him at his home in Aberdeen. Byron

Washington Wilson's photograph of Ballaterach, where the "ill-tricket nickum, Geordie Byron" spent his holidays.

A.U.L. AB78

wrote later about his affection for his cousin, recalling "all we said to each other, all our caresses . ."

Nowadays, the sign at the end of the farm road attracts little attention, yet to anyone interested in Byron it is a fascinating area. Not far from Ballaterach is the farm of Greystone. Isaac Stephen, a local carpenter, had a workshop there and Byron, the "tricket nickum" (mischievious lad), was always nosing around the place.

"TAKKIN' LADDIE"

Isaac's daughter, Mrs Calder, who was married to the farmer at Greystone, described Byron as "a very takkin, laddie, but nae easily managed." He couldn't keep his hands of Isaac's work tools, and reprimands were a waste of time – "he widna tak' a tellin'."

Mrs Calder said that when he was seen coming up the brae from Ballaterach her father would lock the door of his workshop and "gang awa' oot aboot – there wis nae ither way o' daein' wi' him."

Byron's first visit to Deeside was in 1795. He was no budding poet at the time (he said that he "hated poetry" during his school days), but it was while at Ballaterach that he climbed Morven – his "Morven of snow" – and caught his first glimpse of the "dark frowning glories" of Lochnagar.

It was on a later visit to Deeside, when he was about fifteen or sixteen, that he climbed Lochnagar. John Davidson, a ghillie, was his guide. Their route was by the Falls of Garbh Allt and Byron frequently stopped to rest and look at the scenery.

"He was very quiet and did not often speak to me," said David-

son. "When we began to climb the crags of Loch nan Eun I thought he would not be able to scramble up, but he would not have any help from me. When we got to the top he sat a long time on the edge of the rocks looking about him, but seldom asked me any question, and we returned the same way we went up."

THE DREAM

Ballaterach has changed beyond recognition since Byron stayed there, and even since George Washington took his picture, but beyond the farm, where the tracks trail away into the hills, nothing has changed. Here, it is easy to imagine wee Geordie Byron, the "trickit nickum," wandering over the grey-brown moors and looking across the Dee to Lochnagar, dreaming of the day when he would climb that mighty mountain.

Ballaterach today.

Mike Stephen

PANNANICH WELLS HOTEL,

NEAR BALLATER.

R.S.

Chris Norton tests the "miracle" waters at one of the wells at Pannanich.

Loupin' with joy at Pannanich

*I've seen the sick to health return,
I've seen the sad forget to mourn,
I've seen the lame their crutches burn
And loup and fling at Pannanich.*

*I've seen the auld seem young and frisky,
Without the aid of ale or whisky,
I've seen the dullest hearts grow brisky
At blithesome, healthful Pannanich.*

– written last century by a
local poet, John Ogilvy.

When Catherine Byron stayed at Ballaterach with her son George, she occasionally took him to Pannanich Inn, where the Deeside gentry gathered. From there he could look west to the hills, to the new town of Ballater, and across the Dee valley to the ruined kirk of Tullich, sitting in the lap of Morven.

In George Washington Wilson's picture, taken a century later, only a handful of tombstones can be seen in the Tullich churchyard. Now, almost another century on, the cemetery is well filled, and it is still used for burials. The photograph also shows trees growing inside the walls of the kirk, but they have long since gone. The slopes of Pannanich are on left of the picture.

Pannanich and Tullich glower at each other across the valley as if remembering the days when they competed for the crowds who came to be cured by "miracle" waters. In 1760, an old woman suffering from scrofula drank from a spring near Pannanich and bathed her sores in its waters. The "Kings Evil", as the disease was called, disappeared – and Pannanich became the Lourdes of Deeside.

FOUR WELLS

There were four wells on Pannanich, and when the water from them was analysed it was discovered that they were rich in iron. Francis Farquharson, the laird of Monaltrie, built an inn on Pannanich, installed bath-houses, and sparked off a health boom that brought people flocking to Deeside. They crossed the Dee to Pannanich by ferry, but Tullich was unable to cope. In 1783 a bridge was built over the river and Ballater began to take shape.

While Ballater grew, Tullich declined. Its market, its post office and its inn, known as

When a "miracle" came to Deeside

the Change-house at the Stile of Tullich, disappeared.

Over on the other side of the Dee, the fashionable members of society lived in comfort at the new inn, while the less fortunate caught the water as it trickled down the hill. In 1793, a surgeon advertised in the *Aberdeen Journal* that he would "attend at the wells every week", and would call on his convalescent patients, who were scattered in different hamlets "for the benefit of the goat milk."

George Byron and his mother were there some thirty-five years after the wells were discovered. "I was sent to drink goat's *fey* in 1795-1796, in consequence of a threatened decline after scarlet fever," he wrote. Whether or not his recovery was due to the "miracle" waters or the goat's milk was never disclosed.

In recent years, Pannanich Inn has had fluctuating fortunes, being shut down for long periods. Now it has been renovated and re-opened by Chris Norton, a designer from Purley, London, and his wife Vallerie, who have attempted to recapture some of the old spa atmosphere. The emphasis is on luxury.

Chris is also out to promote Pannanich's "miracle" water. He shies away from any suggestion that it is a miraculous cure for people's ills, but he strongly believes that, with its iron

content, it is good for your health. He has had the water analysed and the verdict was that it is "of excellent quality," People with arthritis have been coming to Pannanich to drink it.

The two wells at the back of the inn have been tidied up and the stone bath in the grounds is to be repaired. In the old days, the poor people had a dip in the bath, while the gentry went to the bath-house at the inn. When Queen Victoria visited Pannanich in 1870 she mentioned the outdoor bath.

STABLE-BOY

"We got out and tasted the water, which is strongly impregnated with iron," she wrote in her *Journal*, "and looked at the bath and at the humble but very clean accommodation in the curious little old inn, which used to be much frequented. Brown formerly stayed there for a year as a servant, and then quantities of horses and goats were there."

Brown was a stable-boy at Pannanich before going to Balmoral. The stables are still there, for horse-riding is on of the activities on offer at this "little old inn."

Sightseeing tours of the North-east's whisky trails are laid on for visitors, but, with or without a dram, it looks as if hearts will once again grow brisky at Pannanich.

This lovely view of the River Dee was taken by G.W.W. looking upstream to Craigendarroch and the Pass of Ballater. Today, the view is obscured by trees.

THE QUEEN AT BALLATER, SEPTEMBER, 1897   12,447   G.W.W.

ROYAL LINE

Queen Victoria arrives at Ballater Station in September, 1897. The guard of honour is drawn up, crowds fill the Station Square, and a few loyal subjects doff their bowlers and bonnets.

The Queen, however, was never very keen on travelling on the Royal line to Deeside. She had a fear of rail travel. In 1896, her equerry was instructed to check conditions between Ballater and Windsor. He told the railway authorities to ensure that the line had not "suffered in any way by recent rains and winds."

There was always a pilot train running ahead of the Royal train, carrying its own fitters, lampmen and greasers.

Nowadays, the Royal Family usually fly to Aberdeen Airport and make their way to Balmoral by road.

Ballater Station Square today.

THIS PLAQUE, presented by the Great North of Scotland Railway Association to the Kincardine and Deeside District Council, commemorates the re-building of Ballater Station in 1886, when the Royal Waiting Room behind this wall was opened for Queen Victoria's use.

Ballater Station, for over a century, was the scene of Royal arrivals and departures through six reigns from Queen Victoria to Queen Elizabeth. Many heads of government, and other public figures, arrived at the station on their way to Balmoral Castle.

Mike Stephen

THE ALBERT MEMORIAL HALL, BALLATER.   1222.   G.W.W.

The Albert Memorial Hall in the Station Square at Ballater. There was no memorial plaque to "Albert the Good" above the door of the hall when Washington Wilson took this picture. The photograph on the previous page shows the tribute to "A Prince Indeed." On the other side of the street, a small plaque on the station wall commemorates the rebuilding of the Royal Waiting Room in 1886.

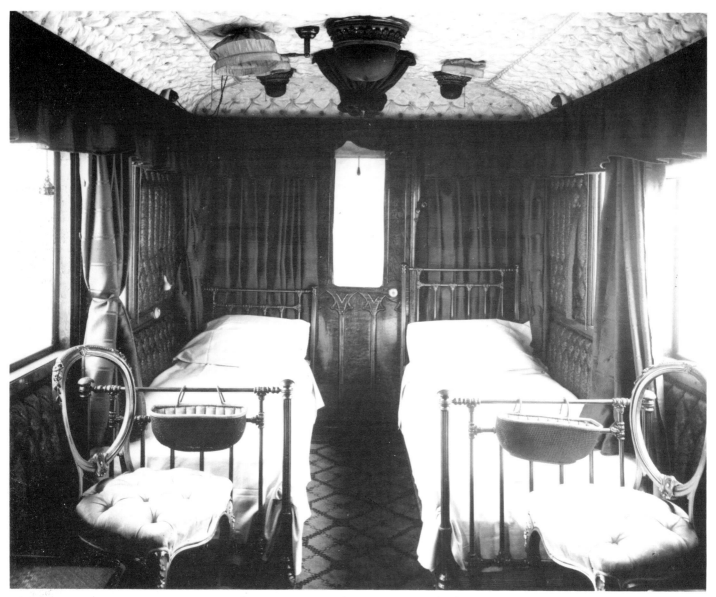

Queen Victoria's bedroom in the Royal saloon.

Palace on wheels

Palace on wheels – that's one description that has been given to the Royal train on which Queen Victoria made the long journey north from Windsor to her Scottish holiday home on Deeside.

She may not have been fond of rail travel, but everything was done to make her comfortable. The coaches on which the Queen and members of the Royal Family travelled were designed to meet their wishes.

Victoria's bedroom on the Royal saloon is seen in the picture above. One of the beds is smaller than the other and it is thought that this was for any of the princesses who were accompanying her.

There was a day and night saloon for the Queen, separated by a toilet area. A small four-seater compartment was provided for a retainer; it

was used both by John Brown and the Munshi – Hafiz Abdul Karim – the Queen's Indian servant.

After John Brown's death, tea-brewing equipment was installed. The Queen refused to eat on the train, stopping at special stations for her

meals, but she had no objection to a cup of tea.

She could never have spilled her cuppa, for she objected to the train travelling at any speed over forty miles an hour. The first saloon built for her had a dial and lever operating a signal on the roof of the carriage, indicating that her Majesty wanted the driver to "go slow" or "stop."

John Brown kept an eye on things. On one occasion he got off at a station, went up to the driver's cabin, and told him angrily that the train was "shakin' like the very devil."

When there was a threat of Fenian attacks on the train, guards checked out all the railway bridges.

Note: The pictures above and on Page 47 are published by kind permission of the National Railway Museum in York.

Down the line . . .

Aboyne – *The train station at Aboyne as it was in its Victorian hey-day.*

Cults – *The busy station at Cults, used at one time by the "subbie" trains.*

Cambus o' May station, now an attractive holiday cottage.

Cutaway Cottage.

National Railway Museum

End of the line

It was almost "the end of the line" for Victoria's reign when the picture above was taken. It shows the crew of the Queen's Royal train before it set off on its final trip from Ballater to Windsor on 5 November, 1900.

"Keep well till I come back," the Queen said, but less than three months later, on 22 January, 1901, she died.

Now the line itself has gone. The Queen resisted any attempt to extend it beyond Ballater, where it would have invaded her privacy at Balmoral, but she could never have thought that one day it would no longer be part of the Deeside scene.

As the plaque at Ballater Station says, it has seen Royal arrivals and departures through six reigns from Queen Victoria to Queen Elizabeth. Now all that is left is a walk-way where people stroll with their dogs.

Mike Stephen

Welcome to Royal Ballater

Ballater is very much a Royal burgh. It is on Balmoral's doorstep, supplies the castle with goods from its shops (it has more "By Appointment" signs than any other village on Deeside) and is frequently visited by members of the Royal Family on private shopping expeditions.

Queen Victoria helped to put Ballater on the map. When she died, the village put out flags for the new monarch, King Edward VII. When he came to Balmoral for the first time as King in September, 1901, he passed through a magnificent "Welcome" arch on the outskirts of the village, near the railway station.

The picture below was taken by Royal photographer Robert Milne, whose studio was beside the arch.

R.S.

Erected in honour of H.M. King Edward VII on his first visit to Balmoral as King. Sept 1901

A.C.

BALLATER, FROM CRAIGENDARROCH. 11,480. G.W.W.

A.U.L. A95

Hilltop look at Ballater

This view of Ballater by George Washington Wilson was taken from Craigendarroch.

The railway station and the Albert Memorial Hall can be seen on the left, but there was no Victoria Hall at that time. Glenmuick Church, the village square, and the main streets can be picked out, while across the River Dee a track pushes its way up Craig Coillich.

The Bridge of Dee, seen clearly in Wilson's picture, was photographed at an earlier stage – at the laying of the arch stones in June, 1885. The bridge was opened in November of that year by Queen Victoria.

The historic bridge picture was taken by the photographer William Watson.

A.C.

Wilson pictures of old thatched cottages of Coilacreich.

A.U.L. D191

The Coillies

Coilacreich Inn.

Mike Stephen

The area around Coilacreich Inn, west of Ballater, was at one time known as the Coillies.

There is a Coilacreich Brae and a Coilacreich Wuid. The Coillies wood is well-known for its birch trees although no one has written a song about it (see Page 69). The spelling of the name has changed over the years, and its meaning is uncertain. One suggestion is that it has a link with the aspen tree.

Kylacreich (Coill a chrich) is one version of the name. This was the spelling given in "Place Names of West Aberdeenshire," and the explanation of it there was "wood of the boundary."

There is a curious and puzzling local saying which goes, "Kyle a creich, faur the soo gae'd the last screech."

Coilacreich Inn, which lies less than two miles from the Brig o' Gairn, was an important coaching inn.

Brig of Gairn.

A.U.L. E452

GETTING ABOUT
– how they once travelled on Deeside

John Milne on his penny-farthing bike.

Bikes, bows and a very special car

John Milne, of Aboyne, was the sort of man who would try his hand at anything. One minute he would be pedalling along as if riding a penny-farthing bike was the easiest thing in the world (see opposite page), the next, having changed his bonnet for a trilby, he would be sitting at the wheel of a car with two pretty girls.

With bows on their hats like that, the girls were something special, but the car was even more special. It was the first car to be driven in Aboyne – the date, August 1901.

John's son was Robert Milne, the Royal photographer, who took many pictures of Queen Victoria and the Royal Family at Balmoral. He once said he regarded the Queen as a friend.

The two cars in the lower photograph were also seen in Aboyne. One was driven by a Mr Canning (left), the other by a Mr Cecil.

The group below thought it was healthier – and more fun – going by bike. The dog seemed to like it. Note, incidentally, the gentleman with the spats!

A.C.

A.C.

There were coaches of all shapes and sizes at this gathering in Ballater's Station Square. No indication is given of why they were there and where they were going, but it must have been a colourful outing.

From horse-drawn coaches to motor coaches. This magnificent charabanc, forerunner to the touring buses that crowd Deeside roads today, operated between Ballater and Braemar. They were already catering for Royal sightseers, for the notice board indicates a stop at Balmoral.

Picture by courtesy of Grampian Transport Museum.

So this is riding side saddle!

Mules were often used to pull carriages in the grounds of Balmoral Castle. In the picture above, Geordie Gordon, a ghillie with Queen Victoria, is seen driving a dog-cart up the main avenue to the castle.

Today, an old milk-float has been converted to carry visitors from the entrance gates up the avenue.

The happy bairn on the right gives a new meaning to the business of riding side-saddle. Who she was is a mystery, but she must have been a junior V.I.P. before she was given a top-hatted retainer to look after her.

It is thought that the picture was taken in the grounds of Balmoral.

Strachan's was a big name in the coaching business in Deeside. The notice board above advertised their summer tours, departing daily from Strachan's garage in Ballater.

Tour No. 6 offered a wonderful trip to the Toll o' Mossat and Alford, returning by Craigievar Castle and Cambus o' May. The return fare was six shillings!

Tourists going to Alford today can still see the bus below and the notice board, for these pictures of them are featured at the Grampian Transport Museum.

Pictures by courtesy of Grampian Transport Museum.

PASS
OF
BALLATER

The Pass of Ballater last century.

The Fog-house in the Pass.

Tea in the Fog-house

A short distance through the Pass of Ballater from the main Aberdeen road an old ruin can be seen behind the dyke, not far from where the Monaltrie road comes into the pass. This is all that remains of a fog-house that stood there early last century.

The word "fog" means moss, and a fog-house was a summer house lined with moss. The Ballater one was made of granite and the picture on the left shows what it looked like. The picture is from a water colour painted by Peter Cleland, who was an Aberdeen art master from 1847 to 1867.

Tea parties were often held in the fog-house, which was said to be tastefully furnished inside.

There was also a popular fog-house at the Falls of Garbh-allt near Invercauld. See Page 89.

Monaltrie House, with the Crags of Ballater in the background. The picture was taken by George Washington Wilson, who also took the photograph below. This rock face has become a practice ground for climbers.

S OF BALLATER. 2708. G.W.

Scaling the heights of the Yellow Crag

R.S.

High above the Pass of Ballater, a pair of climbers rest on their last push up the crags of Sgur Bui-dhe – the Yellow Crag or Hill.

The old name of the Pass was the Crags (or Craigs) of Ballater. There are various historical references to the Crags of Ballater and a Roman road is said to have gone from the Crags of Ballater towards Corgarff.

The old Deeside Road went from Tullich through the Pass of Ballater and crossed the Gairn by an ancient pack-horse bridge.

Lead, and even silver, was quarried above the Pass, as well as stone for building. The small stone bridge over the Loin Burn was built as an access to the quarries. The fog-house was made of granite from the quarry nearby.

Before Ballater was built, the old highway had a link with the ford and ferry over the River Dee, near where the present bridge stands today.

There was also an old church road which came over the west shoulder of Creagan Riach and down to the Pass a short distance east of the entrance to Monaltrie House.

There is a fanciful story that the Black Colonel of Inverey, hunted by red-coats, scaled the Crags of Ballater and escaped. "If we had known he could fly as well as run," said one red-coat, "we might have spared ourselves the roughest ride I ever had."

The old Kirk Road from Easter Morven, which was a right-of-way, ran down to the Pass and continued to the grounds of Monaltrie.

Balmearach is a farm in the Pass and west of it, on a site overlooking the Pass, are the ruins of Gairn Castle, a long-forgotten hunting-seat of the Forbeses.

GATEWAY TO GLENMUICK

BRIDGE OF MUICK, BALLATER. 2535. G.W.W.

The old Bridge of Muick is the gateway to a glen that today draws thousands of visitors along the winding road to the Spittal of Muick, where drovers once rested before pushing over the Capel Mounth to Glen Clova and the south. The road to the Spittal passes Birkhall, the Queen Mother's Deeside home, and the Mill of Sterin. Sterin, from stairean, meaning stepping stones, was the original name of Birkhall. It was there that Queen Victoria crossed the ford on her way into the hills. Farther on are the tumbling waters of the Linn of Muick, whose pool, according to the traveller Thomas Pennant, was "supposed by the vulgar to be bottomless." On the right of Washington Wilson's picture is the old churchyard of Glenmuick, where there is a rough gravestone with the name John Mitchell on it. He is said to have lived from 1596 to 1722, making him 126 years old. There is also a memorial plaque and seat commemorating Queen Victoria's inspection of the Gordon Highlanders at Bridgend of Muick in 1899 before they left for the South African war.

QUEEN VICTORIA AT BIRKHALL

The Inch Bobbard of Queen Victoria's "Journal" is Inchnabobart, a farm on the west side of the River Dee. The Queen, on her way to the Dubh Loch, had come over the hills from Easter Balmoral and moved down the Dee by Inchnabobart to Birkhall, fording the river before travelling on to Alltna-giubhsaich.

Birkhall, in its lovely setting in Glenmuick, is the home of the Queen Mother. Here she fishes – and here she taught Prince Charles the art of angling.

Birkhall House and its estate of 6500 acres was bought from the Gordons by Queen Victoria for the Prince of Wales, but was sold back to the Queen in 1885.

Behind it are the familiar Coyles of Muick. Joseph Gordon of Birkhall, who was "out" in the '45 Jacobite Rising, hid out in the Coyles at a spot known as "The Laird's Bed."

Mr Whytt (White) and Mr Brown sheltered from the Redcoats at Birkhall. They were the Oliphants of Gask, father and son, who took refuge at Birkhall after fleeing from Culloden. They were friends of Joseph Gordon and his wife Elizabeth.

Mr White and Mr Brown eventually succeeded in leaving the country and settled in Sweden. Elizabeth Gordon wrote to Lady Gask: "I rec'd a letter from a gentleman, written from Gottenborg, who writes me, Mr White and Mr Brown is in very good health."

Birkhall was built in 1715 by Charles and Rachel Gordon. An inscription over the doorway reads "17 C.G.R.G. 15".

BIRKHALL GLENMUICK, 48, G.W.W.

A.U.L. E3363

60

When seven sons died at Knock

The ruins of Knock Castle stand on a tree-shaded knoll a short distance west of the Brig o' Muick, on the road that leads past Abergeldie Castle and on to the gates of Balmoral.

It was once a keep of considerable strength, strategically placed, but there is nothing in its pleasant setting to hint at its gory past.

The tower was built in 1600, although there was an earlier building on the same site. The 4th Earl of Huntly granted the lands and Castle of Knock to a brother of the Gordon laird of nearby Abergeldie.

There was continual feuding between the Gordons of Abergeldie and the Forbeses of Strathgirnock, whose land separated Knock and Abergeldie. The seven sons of Alexander Gordon, who built the 17th century castle, were casting peats when they were attacked and slain by a party of Forbes from Strathgirnock.

The Forbeses cut off the heads of the seven men, tied them to the cross tops of the flaughter spades, and stuck the implements in the ground. When Alexander Gordon was given the news he fell over the stair banister in Knock Castle and was killed.

Brave Braikley's yetts . . . .

"Inverey cam doun Deeside, whistlin and playin,
He was at brave Braikley's yetts ere it was dawin."

Braickley House, or Brackley House, as G.W.W. called it. It is now known as the House of Glenmuick. The Castle of Braickley features in a well-known ballad.

GLENMUICK HOUSE FROM N. BALLATER 1815 G.W.W.

House on the Muick

The corner of Deeside where the River Muick runs into the Dee was once dominated by a huge house set on a hillside at the mouth of the glen.

The building was Glenmuick House, built about 1870 for Sir James Mackenzie. It could be seen for miles around. The picture above shows George Washington Wilson's view of it, looking across a curving bend of the Dee.

The estate of Glenmuick was originally part of the Deeside possessions of the Huntly Gordons. It was acquired by John Farquharson of Invercauld in 1749 and sold in 1868 by Colonel James Ross Farquharson to Mr (later Sir) James Mackenzie, the son of an Aberdeen silk merchant, who made a fortune in India.

Glenmuick House was designed by Sir Samuel Morton Peto, a contractor and politician, who was one of the sponsors of Prince Albert's Great

Exhibition in 1851. Built of granite, it formed three sides of a square, with the north wing surmounted by a 75ft. high tower.

One writer, John Macintosh, said it had "an exceedingly attractive appearance," but Nigel Tranter described it as "a great sham-Tudor edifice," adding that its eventual demolition was "no loss."

The Shah of Persia stayed at Glenmuick House during his visit to Deeside, and the Tsar of

Russia, who stayed at Balmoral in 1896, paid a visit to Glenmuick House to see Lord Glenesk, who was then the shooting tenent.

Braickly House (see opposite page) is now known as the House of Glenmuick.

The name Braickley (or Brackley) has a link with the ballad "The Baron of Braickley," which tells how John Farquharson, the Black Colonel of Inverey (see Page 112) came to Braickley, goaded the laird, John Gordon, into coming to the yetts (gates), and killed him – "the Baronne of Braikley is dead and awa."

There are four different versions of the ballad, which is said to mix up at least two different events. The actual setting of the ballad was another Braickley – the long-vanished Castle of Braickley, which stood near the site of the present building.

When a lovely chapel died . . .

The picture below shows a lovely Deeside chapel, but today no one can worship in it – or even see it. It was torn down, some of its granite blocks going to build shooting butts on the surrounding moors, and all that remains is the tower, rising forlornly among the trees below the House of Glenmuick.

Few people even know that the ruin is there. It is all that is left of the Episcopal church of St. Nathalan's, built in 1875 by Sir James Mackenzie.

The dykes around it have partly collapsed. Sir James built a vault beside the church and several members of his family are interred there. Near it is a monument to Sir James – Born 1818, Died 1890.

On the opposite side of the church is a fenced-in burial ground, where simple crosses mark the graves of other Mackenzies, many of them military men.

GLENMUICK CHAPEL BALLATER. 3037. G.W.W.

A.U.L. C1049

63

The ruins of Glenmuick chapel – and in the foreground a simple cross marks a Mackenzie grave.

R.S.

Looking across Loch Muick . . .

Looking across Loch Muick to Glass-allt Shiel, built by Queen Victoria. She wrote in her "Journal" in October, 1868, that it looked cheerful and comfortable." The picture was taken by William Watson. Note the boat drawn up on the shore of the loch. Below is the building that stood there in 1862, before her new shiel was erected.

So cozy and nice . . .

We arrived at half-past six at the Glassalt Shiel, which looked so cheerful and comfortable, all lit up, and the rooms so cozy and nice. There is a wonderful deal of room in the compact little house. A good staircase (the only one) leads to the upper floor.

We dined at about half-past eight in the small dining room. This over, after waiting for a little in my sitting room, Brown came to say all the servants were ready for the house-warming, and at twenty minutes to ten we went into the little dining room, which had been cleared, and where all the servants were assembled.

– From Queen Victoria's "Journal".

. . . to the first Widow's House

THE GLASSALT SHIEL, LOCH MUICK. 2530 G.W.W.

A.U.L. B662

Glass-allt Shiel has changed little since this picture was taken by George Washington Wilson more than a century ago. There were nineteen people at Glass-allt on Queen Victoria's first visit there. The number included a policeman, who said the Queen, "only comes to do duty outside at night."

Victoria seldom let the affairs of state interfere with her visits to Glass-allt. When there were complaints about her refusal to entertain the King of Denmark on one occasion, Sir Henry Ponsonby, her Private Secretary, said, "She has gone to Glassalt and there is an end to all arguments."

Glassalt Shiel was built seven years after the death of Prince Albert. Before that, their favourite shiel had been "The Hut" at Alltna-guibhsaich.

I thought of my darling husband

After the first reel, "whisky-toddy" was brought round for every one, and Brown begged I would drink to the "fire-kindling." Then Grant made a little speech, with an allusion to the wild place we were in, and concluding with a wish "that our Royal mistress, our good Queen" should live long.

I thought of the happy past and my darling husband whom I fancied I must see, and who always wished to build here, in this favourite wild spot, quite in amidst the hills. At Altnagiuthasach I could not have lived again now – alone. It is far better to have built a totally new house; but then the sad thought struck me that it was the first Widow's House.

– From Queen Victoria's "Journal".

Royal Retreats

In her early years at Balmoral, Queen Victoria often slept in a cottage near Loch Muick know as "the Hut." The Queen's sketch of this "most commodious cottage" is shown on the right. Allt-na-guibhsaich wasn't always commodious. At one time it was a sod-covered, one-chimney building.

Victoria, who stayed at "the Hut" with Prince Albert after a day in the hills hunting deer, called it "our humble little abode." It was there that members of the Royal Family held torchlight dances on the lawn.

The picture below shows Allt-na-guibhsaich as George Washington Wilson's camera portrayed it, while the lower picture shows it as it is today. Members of the Royal Family no longer stay in it, but it is used by staff when the Queen is staying at Balmoral.

It is a familiar landmark to hill-walkers tramping along the road from the Spittal of Glen Muick on their way to climb Lochnagar.

Allt-na-guibhsaich (GWW)

A.U.L. F4279

Allt-na-guibhsaich today

R.S.

THE DHU LOCH. GLEN MUICK. 2548. G.W.W.

A.U.L. B1325

On September 11, 1849, Queen Victoria and Prince Albert went on a trip over the hills to the Dubh Loch — the Dark Loch — seen above in Washington Wilson's photograph. They started from "The Hut" at Alt-na-guibhsaich and ended the day with a rough trip on Loch Muick. This is what the Queen wrote in her diary about the outing —

Over the hills to the Dubh Loch

It was half-past twelve when we began ascending the hill immediately behind the house, and proceeded along over the hills, to a great height, whence the view was very fine, quite overhanging the loch, and commanding an extensive view of Loch Muick beyond the opposite side.

The road got worse and worse. It was particularly bad when we had to pass the Burn of the Glassalt, which falls into the loch, and was very full. There had been so much rain that the burns and rivers were very full and the ground was quite soft. We rode over the Strone Hill, the wind blowing dreadfully hard when we came to the top.

Albert walked almost from the first, and shot a hare and a grouse; he put up a good many of them. We walked to a little hollow immediately above the Dhu Loch, and at half-past three seated ourselves there and had some very welcome luncheon. The loch is only a mile in length, and very wild; the hills, which are very rocky and precipitous, rising perpendicularly from it.

In about half an hour we began our journey homewards. We came straight down beside Muick, which falls in the most beautiful way over the rocks and stones in the glen. We rode down and only had to get off to cross the Glassalt, which was an awkward ford to scramble over.

The road was rough, but certainly far less soft and disagreeable than the one we came by. I rode "Lochnagar" at first, but changed him for Colonel Gordon's pony, as I thought he took fright at bogs.

We were only an hour coming down to the boat. The evening was very fine, but it blew very hard on the lake and the men could not pull, and I got so alarmed that I begged to land. We accordingly landed and rode home along a sort of sheep-path on the side of the lake; we had

seven hundred feet above us, and I suppose one hundred feet below. However, we arrived at the hut quite safely at twenty minutes to seven, thankful to have got through all our difficulties and adventures.

Old John Gordon amused Albert by saying, in speaking of the bad road we had gone, "It's something steep and something rough," and "this is the only best," meaning that it was very bad — which was a characteristic reply.

68

ABERGELDIE CASTLE FROM N·E· 656· G·W·W·

THE BIRKS O' ABERGELDIE

— Toasted in birch wine!

Bonnie lassie, will ye go,
Will ye go, will ye go,
Bonnie lassie, will ye go
To the Birks o' Abergeldie?

Ye shall get a gown o' silk,
A gown o' silk, a gown o' silk,
Ye shall get a gown o' silk,
And a coat of callimankie.

Although the distillery on the doorstep of Balmoral Castle is well-known for its Royal Lochnagar whisky, another castle two miles away has links with a drink that in its day was no less famous – birch wine.

Birch wine, like Abergeldie birches themselves, had a big reputation on Deeside. One report said that it was "superior to the finest champagne." The last record of its use at Abergeldie Castle was in 1831, when the laird died, but some

time after that – in 1845 – it was selling at Birkhall for a shilling a bottle.

Of course, if you drunk birch wine that tasted like champagne you dressed for the occasion, probably in a coat of callimankie. Callimankie, or calamanco, was a glossy woollen fabric woven with a checked design that showed only on one side.

Rabbie Burns shed the callimankie coat when he took "The Birks of Abergeldie" and turned it into "The Birks of Aberfeldy." A Burns writer said a few years back that during a visit to Aberfeldy the poet "composed the jaunty 'Birks of Aberfeldy' on the spot."

The truth is that Rabbie based his Aberfeldy piece on the much older Abergeldie air. One critic said that

he transferred the scenery as well, for at that time there were no birches at Aberfeldy.

"The 'Birks of Aberfeldy' have no right to the name or the song either," wrote George Walker. "Had Burns seen the birch trees here he would not have thought the Aberfeldy ones worthy of the honour."

Where they burned Kitty Rankine

Abergeldie Castle is seen fleetingly by motorists as they roar up Deeside on their way to more important castles like Balmoral and Braemar. It sits on the south bank of the Dee, screened by trees, and if you want to see it properly you have to cross the river and climb a hill called Creag nam Ban.

There are two reasons why Creag nam Ban is the best viewpoint. One is that it offers an excellent bird's-eye view of this 16th century tower-house. The other is that it has a ghoulish connection with the castle. They threw witches into the dungeon there and then burned them on top of the hill.

The name Creag nam Ban means "the women's crag," but it is better known as the Witches Hill. Fact and fiction get mixed up when the story is told. Witches were certainly burned on the summit (they once pointed out the hollow where the stake was fixed), but the tale of Kitty Rankine has to be treated with a pinch of salt.

FRENCH KATE

Kitty Rankie or Rankine – French Kate – was a maid at Abergeldie who is said to have dabbled in black magic and ended up on Creag nam Ban. George VI stayed at Abergeldie Castle and his brother Bertie (Edward VIII) thought that its bat-infested tower was haunted by Kitty Rankine's ghost.

There is a hoary old story about how a witch and a warlock were both condemned to death and imprisoned in Abergeldie Castle. The witch escaped and the warlock offered to recapture her if he was pardoned. She turned herself into a hare, but the warlock immediately changed himself into a greyhound. He had almost caught the hare when it became a mouse and disappeared into a dyke, but the clever warlock turned himself into a weasel and caught the witch.

So if you ever see a hare on Creag nam Ban . . . . or a mouse . . . . or a weasel . . . . well, you can never be sure, can you?

The Gordons built Abergeldie about 1550 and have owned it ever since, though they leased it to the Royal Family for over a century.

Until a bridge was built over the

The bridge and castle today.

R.S.

Dee from the North Deeside Road to the castle, the only way to get across the river was by a rope and cradle "bridge." It was a Heath Robinson affair that inspired awe, and a measure of disbelief, in anyone who saw it. It amounted to little more than a big box balanced between two lines of rope. The "cradle" was guided over the river by a guy rope.

Not surprisingly, there were a number of accidents. An Exciseman hot on the trail of whisky smugglers lost his life when the rope broke while the river was in flood.

The worst accident took place in 1824, when a newly-married couple, Peter Frankie, a gamekeeper at Allt-na-giubhsaich, and his bride, Barbara Brown, from Crathienaird, were drowned on their wedding day.

THE CRADLE

There is an interesting footnote to the story of the Abergeldie "cradle." The local postman used it to send his letters across the river to the castle. John Fyfe, the Aberdeen Granite Merchant, saw the "postie" doing this and struck on the idea of building a cableway for quarry work instead of cranes.

He called the new cableway a Blondin after Charles Blondin, the tight-rope walker, and the first Blondin was erected at his Kemnay quarry in 1873. Other cableway Blondins sprang up in quarries all over Scotland.

A suspension footbridge was built at Abergeldie in 1885 and the old "box" bridge disappeared. Today, there is a "Private" sign on the bridge at its north end, but it is superfluous. The gate there is locked and the bridge is falling into disrepair, with parts of its wooden walkway missing. It looks more dangerous now than the cradle bridge must have looked last century.

So, if you want to get to Abergeldie from the North Deeside Road you go there by car . . . . or build a "box" and get yourself a long piece of rope.

A pony grazes in a field on the Balmoral estate. Behind, set against the background of the Deeside hills, is Crathie Church, which draws thousands of sightseers when the Queen and the Royal Family are in residence at Balmoral Castle.

A.U.L. D2282

Hundreds of onlookers gathered at Crathie on September 11, 1893, to watch Queen Victoria lay the foundation stone of Crathie Church. The ceremony is pictured below right.

Less than 2 years later, the Queen returned to the red-roofed kirk on the hillside at Crathie to dedicate the new church. The date was Tuesday, June 18, 1895, and the weather was cold and blustery.

George Washington Wilson took this shot of the church from higher up the hill, looking down on the rear of the building. In the distance, just left of the kirk spire, is Prince Albert's memorial cairn, a well-known landmark on Deeside.

The memorial pyramid on Craig Lowrigan (below left) is 35ft. high and has a 40ft.-wide base. The inscription on it records that it was raised by Albert's "broken-hearted widow." It carries lines from "Wisdom of Solomon" – "He being made perfect in a short time fulfilled a long time."

R.S.

A.C.

BALMORAL CASTLE, FROM S.W.   10,164.   G.W.V.

A lovely winter scene at Balmoral Castle, showing the Royal home on Deeside as few visitors ever see it.

73

Sixty glorious years

Sixty glorious years . . . and a huge "Welcome" arch smothers the entrance gateway to Balmoral Castle in preparation for Queen Victoria's arrival at her Deeside home.

The date was May, 1897, and it was her birthday. "My poor old birthday again came round," she wrote, "and it seems sadder each year. Seventy-eight is a good age."

She noted in her diary that "the telegrams began to pour in in a most extraordinary manner, and this continued till late that night, not only from all relations, connections, and friends, but from all sorts of individuals, Public Bodies, Societies, etc."

Her Diamond Jubilee was celebrated in June and bonfires blazed on hilltops throughout Scotland.

Even though seventy-eight was "a good age," Victoria was still fussy about her appearance. On a drive to Crathie Church, Lady Lytton noticed that she took care that her hair did not get ruffled.

LOCH-NA-GAR, FROM NEAR BALMORAL. 1192. G.W.W.

Dark Lochnagar

Lochnagar – it dominates the Deeside landscape. George Washington Wilson used it as a backdrop to a number of his pictures . . . Lochnagar from Bush, which John Brown's father farmed; from the Home Farm at Balmoral; and in the distance behind Prince Albert's memorial cairn.

He also photographed its hard, craggy face from above the loch which gave it its name.

The top picture shows the bridge over the Dee from Crathie to Balmoral, with the South Deeside Road going east towards Easter Balmoral. In the extreme right is the dairy and in front of it is what is now the golf course, running down across the road to the river.

● see opposite page

Top – Lochnagar from Bush. Bottom – Home Farm, Balmoral, looking to Lochnagar.

The charm of Deeside . . .

STERS HOUSE, BALMORAL. 4553 G.W.W.

A.U.L. C1028

The charm of Royal Deeside is strikingly captured in the George Washington Wilson pictures on these pages. In the photograph above, Wilson's camera roamed over the River Dee to the distant hills, using the West Lodge and Forester's House on the Balmoral estate as his focal point.

. . . in its Royal setting

Winding roads and a winding river . . . and Balmoral Castle caught between them like a jewel in a silver setting. Wilson took this picture of the castle from Craig Nordie, which rises near Carn na Cuimhne, the assembly cairn for the Farquharson clan in time of trouble. Craig Nordie is from Creag an Orduigh, meaning the rock of command.

A.U.L. C6043

The Castle Ballroom at Balmoral. The ballroom, with its timbered ceiling and Gothic chandeliers, is the only part of Balmoral Castle open to the public. Exhibitions of paintings and porcelain, silver trophies and notes and sketches done by Queen Victoria, are held there during the summer months. The ballroom is 68ft. by 25ft. The original ballroom, called the Iron Ballroom, was a metal construction first seen by Prince Albert at the Great Exhibition in 1851.

John Brown's lucky threepenny

A close-up of John Brown's watch chain. The Queen Victoria lucky threepenny is top left. Under it is a medallion, while on the right is a miniture pipe.

R.S.

One thing is missing from the Royal treasures and momentoes that go on public display in the Ballroom at Balmoral Castle each summer – John Brown's lucky threepenny.

Paintings of Queen Victoria's controversial Royal retainer have been put on show in the Ballroom in the past (exhibits change from time to time), but no one has ever seen Brown's lucky threepenny piece. No one, in fact, knows what happened to it.

So, if you want to have a look at the threepenny bit you have to go for a walk in the Balmoral woods.

After Brown's death, Victoria commissioned a life-size statue of him by Edgar Boehm. Brown had always called the Vienna-born sculptor Mr Bum. What he thought of his commission remains unrecorded, for it was Brown who complained to the Queen that her hill ponies were being ridden to death by Boehm and others. Boehm threatened to leave Balmoral.

Nevertheless, the statue was completed, carrying the inscription on its plinth, "Friend more than Servant, Loyal, Truthful, Brave, Selfless than Duty, even to the Grave."

It stood for a long time beside the Garden Cottage in which the Queen often worked on her despatch boxes, with Brown watching over her. Now he had gone, but with the statue outside the door he was still there in spirit — too much in spirit, as far as some of the estate workers were concerned.

LIFE-LIKE

The statue was so life-like that the more superstitious members of the Royal staff kept well away from it in daylight and crossed themselves when they were forced to pass it after dark.

When Queen Victoria died, the Prince of Wales (now Edward VII) attempted to wipe out everything that reminded him of Brown. Busts of him were smashed and photographs burned. In addition, Boehm's statue was banished to a corner of Balmoral behind the dairy.

It is still there today, hemmed in by fir trees and larches, well away from the castle. Visitors have difficulty finding the statue.

You would almost think that he had a smile on his face, musing, perhaps, on how he had held his own against Mr. Bum, the Prince of Wales, and all his other enemies at Court. The only thing that mattered to him was what the Queen thought of him, and the two medals on his broad chest testified to that.

One was the Faithful Serveant Medal, the other the Devoted Service Medal. Both sparked off fresh rows about Brown's relationship with the Queen.

The Devoted Service Medal, carried a £25 annuity for life. Brown became the first – and last – recipient of the award. The cynics called it the Greater Order of Brown.

Both the Devoted Service Medal and the Faithful Servant Medal are shown in Boehm's statue. The sculptor was meticul-ous in his work, for the smallest detail in tunic, sporran, bonnet and shoes is brought out in the statue. Mr Bum also sculpted John Brown's lucky threepenny.

CHARMS

The threepenny is one of a number of charms strung across Brown's waistcoat — and, of course, it has Queen Victoria's head on one side of it. It was said that carried there because of his feelings for the Queen, in the same way that some people carried pictures in lockets.

The mind boggles at what today's tabloid press would have made of that sentimental little gesture. They would have seen it as proof that there was a special relationship between the Queen and her servant, and they would almost certainly have pointed out that Mr Brown's lucky threepenny hung from an Albert — a type of watch-chain named after the Prince Consort.

Children of the Mist . . .

This picture of deer, taken against a background of misty hills, was given the title of "Children of the Mist" by George Washington Wilson. It is a remarkable study, taking into account the equipment that Wilson had to use last century.

The photograph on the right shows a less romantic side to life in the wilderness. Here, Wilson's camera has captured the moment when a dead stag is brought down from the hills on the back of a keeper's pony.

Huntin' shootin' and fishin'

Donald Stewart, one of the foresters at Balmoral, with a stag shot by Prince Albert on October 4, 1854, in Corrie-na-Poitch. Reproduced by permission of Her Majesty the Queen.

Although the Deeside landscape often came under the probing eye of Wilson's camera, he made little attempt to photograph its wild life. In George Walker's account of their trip there is a fleeting reference to deer coming down from the hills at dusk, but no mention at all of trying to take pictures of them.

Wilson's landscapes were aimed at the commercial market and the deer that roamed over the Deeside hills were not part of that. It was the domain of the artist, not the photographer. In 1854, when Wilson was taking his first pictures of Balmoral, Edwin Landseer was putting the finishing touches to "Royal Sports on Hill and Loch," which had Loch Muick for a background.

Wilson always claimed to be an artist *and* a photographer and one of his photographs shows what he might have produced if the Monarch of the Glen had been among his subjects. The picture, entitled "Children of the Mist," is a superb study, taken with cumbersome equipment ill-suited for wild life photography.

The trophy was all-important

to the Victorian hunter. Hundreds of stags' heads and antlers decorated the ceilings of Mar Lodge and Glentanar House, as well as the walls and rooms in Balmoral Castle. The "stuffers" (taxidermists) in Braemar were in great demand. The artist Carl Haag was also commissioned to do an oil painting of dead stags being presented to the Queen at the entrance to Balmoral Castle.

When Wilson was at Balmoral in 1854, Prince Albert, along with his keepers, jagers and ghillies, returned triumphantly to the castle with their trophies. Wilson and John Hay, Jun., who was his partner at that time, were asked to record the event. In all these studies the stag is seen laid out at the foot of a tree with a keeper or keepers beside it.

One of the photographs, which

showed John MacDonald, the Prince Consort's Jager with a stag, was used as the basis of an illustration in *Leaves from the Journal of our Life in the Highlands*, which the Queen published in 1868. Many of the line illustrations in the *Journal* were made directly from Wilson's photographs.

Victoria often sketched stags shot by her husband (see above), and the Prince himself tried his hand with pen and sketch-book. "When a stag was heard to roar we all turned into the wood," she wrote. "We heard a shot – then complete silence – and, after another pause of some little time, three more shots. Albert had killed the stag; and on the road he lay, a little way beyond Invergelder – the beauty that we had admired yesterday evening. He was a magnificent animal, and

I sat down and scratched a little sketch of him on a bit of paper that MacDonald had in his pocket."

MacDonald featured in a number of Royal sketches. The Prince did a quick drawing of him (see left) as he lay in the heather watching for deer. Bearded, handsome, he featured prominently in the Landseer painting, "Royal Sports on Hill and Loch."

The Queen gave explicit instructions on how she wanted the grouping for this painting. "It is to be thus: I, stepping out of the boat at Loch Muich, Albert, in his Highland dress, assisting me out, & I am looking at the stag which he is supposed to have just killed. Bertie is on the deer pony with MacDonald (whom Landseer much admires) standing behind, with rifles and plaids on his shoulder."

The Queen wanted the painting to be "singularly dignified, poetical and totally novel." It was certainly novel, but there was nothing dignified about the final change in the tableau. MacDonald ended up holding a fish, not a rifle.

Albert the Hunter

R.S.

Prince Albert's statue.

A.U.L. ABl06

A hunting dog stands at Prince Albert's side in the statue of the Prince Consort in the grounds of Balmoral Castle. Nothing could be more appropriate, for if Balmoral was a "dear Paradise" to Queen Victoria it was a hunter's Paradise to her husband.

There are signs of this all around . . . in the statues of chamois and deer outside the castle and the paintings inside it, in the relief sculpture on the west wall of St. Hubert, the patron saint of hunters, and in the menacing sculpture of the wild boar seen in Washington Wilson's picture. The boar is still there, but it has been moved away from what is now the rose garden.

Albert may have been an enthusiastic hunter, but he was never a good one. The deer he shot were no mighty monarchs of the glen. Some were only five or six stone in weight, and it was even said that he was such a bad shot that he hit the beast at which he wasn't aiming.

Nor was he a good sport. When he was staying at Blair Castle he thought nothing of shooting a semi-tame stag from a castle window, and he even took pot-shots at stags from the Queen's carriage when driving back to Balmoral with her after a day's hunting. Perhaps this was to compensate for a bad day on the hills!

Photographs show him dressed like a gentleman when he went out shooting, which may explain why he was never particularly keen on the crude Scottish practice of crawling about on hands and knees when stalking deer.

There is a memorial to his distaste for such things – the Ditch. When you walk up Glen Gelder and look across the Gel-

der Burn you can see the Ditch, a 4ft. deep half-mile long trench cut out of the moor so that Prince Albert didn't have to go down on all-fours when he was stalking. He simply popped his head up at regular intervals and banged away at the deer.

BALMORAL CASTLE ON THE WEST TERRACE. 712. G.W.W.

A.U.L. AB94

The boar.

By courtesy of Christie's Scotland Limited.

A day on the Deeside moors

The picture above brings to life a day on the moors of Deeside . . . as seen through the eyes and brush of a 19th century painter.

The setting is Glentanar and the familiar figure in the shooting hat is Sir William Cunliffe Brooks, the Laird of Glentanar. With him is Charles Gordon, 11th Marquis of Huntly, while also in the picture is Lord Francis Horace Pierrepoint Cecil.

To the right is a noted ghillie and stalker, Donald McIntosh, while in the dog-cart are three pairs of English setters.

The painting, which is by Carl Suhrlandt, is an oil on canvas and is signed and dated 1889. It was sold by Christie's Scotland Limited at a sale of fine paintings and drawings in April, 1988, in Edinburgh. The price – £16,500.

"Grouse Shooting on the Glentanar Estate" was painted a year before Sir William Cunliffe Brooks bought the estate from the Earl of Huntly's trustees for £120,000. He held a lease of the forest of Glentanar for a number of years before that. W.C.B also bought the estates of Aboyne and Ferrar.

The glen was famous for its fir trees, large quantities being cut and marketed for timber.

R.S.

The gun which Cunliffe Brooks carries in Carl Suhrlandt's painting is a different weapon from the one seen in the picture above. Here, Jimmy Oswald, head keeper on the Glentanar estate, is showing two Danish visitors the type of rifle used by W.C.B. when he hunted an elusive deer which he called the Haunted Stag.

He finally tracked it down and killed it on October 9, 1877, and to mark his success he had two pillars built on the moor where he shot it. They were placed 267 yards apart – the distance at which he brought down his quarry.

Each pillar has a huge stone ball perched on top of a pyramid. On one can be seen the words "The Haunted Stag," while on the second stone is a verse describing how "the sure bullet to its fatal mark hath spread."

Although the gun in the picture isn't the one that shot the Haunted Stag, it is very similar. It is a Martini Henry action weapon made by BSA. It carries the date 1879.

84

BOWLER-HATTED FISHERMAN

The bowler-hatted gentleman casting his line on the River Dee watched by his ghillie is General The Hon. Charles Gray, who was Queen Victoria's private secretary.

Toories and Tammies . . . a fine study of fishers taking a break from their sport on Deeside. They are all dressed for the part, but top marks for style go to the bearded ghillie with the grappling hook.

The Stuffer

Braemar was well-known last century for its taxidermists. They called them stuffers.

Old records show that there was a stuffer at Mar Lodge and another in the village.

Today, the tradition is maintained by Willie Forbes, who was head keeper on the Mar Lodge estate. He is seen (right) with a fox head which he mounted after tracking the fox in the hills that can be seen from his home on the road to the Linn of Dee.

Willie has "stuffed" everything from stags to capercaillies. He once stuffed a salmon caught by Gerald Ford, the President of the United States.

A KING
(and two in the making)
AT GAMES

HIS MAJESTY AT THE BRAEMAR GATHERING. 14,711. G.W.W.

A King and two future Kings are seen in this Washington Wilson picture of the Braemar Gathering at Braemar Castle. King Edward VII, wearing a cape, is pointing out something to the Duke of Fife. Behind is the future King George V, while just outside the Royal Pavillion are Princess Mary and Prince Edward, later King Edward VIII – the Duke of Windsor. The lower picture shows the Princess of Wales arriving at the Gathering when it was held at Balmoral in 1887. The Balmoral Highlanders, with their Lochaber axes and Royal Stewart tartan, formed a Guard of Honour.

BRAEMAR GATHERING—ARRIVAL OF PRINCESS OF WALES. 10,387. G.W.W.

BRAEMAR GATHERING, MAR CASTLE. 11986. G.W.W.

Mar Castle (Braemar Castle) was the setting for this Gathering towards the end of last century. In the picture below it has switched to Balmoral, where, as G.W.W. noted, a young lad was dancing the Sword Dance – the Ghillie-Callum. Unfortunately, most of the people around the dance board have turned their backs on him to watch a burly heavyweight putting the shot.

BRAEMAR GAMES___DANCING GHILLIE-CALLUM. 10,393. G.W.W.

OLD INVERCAULD BRIDGE. BRAEMAR. 10,142. G.W.W.

The Old Invercauld Bridge near Braemar, a scene that has been reproduced in countless paintings and photographs. It became a private bridge when Prince Albert built a new bridge a little distance to the west so that Queen Victoria could retain her privacy at Balmoral.

George Washington Wilson's picture of the Falls of Garbh Allt.

Falls of Garbh Allt

R.S.

"Very grand," said the Queen . . .

Top left – The "bridge to nowhere," spanning the waters of the Garbh Allt.

Right – The small wooden bridge over the lower falls.

R.S.

There is nowhere on Deeside more spectacularly beautiful than the corner of Balmoral where the Falls of Garbh Allt come tumbling down the Dee. They lie in the heart of Ballochbuie, the ancient pine forest which Queen Victoria called "the bonniest plaid in Scotland."

The way to the falls is by a track running through the woods from the old Bridge of Dee. In 1859, Prince Albert built the new Invercauld Bridge and closed the old one to ensure that Queen Victoria had privacy on her Balmoral estate.

After Queen Victoria had climbed Lochnagar in September, 1848, she came down through Ballochbuie woods and had a look at the Falls. "We walked up to the Falls of Garbhalt, which are beauti-

ful," she wrote. "The rocks are very grand, and the view from the little bridge, and also from a seat a little lower down, is extremely pretty.

The Falls are spanned by an impressive metal footbridge. There have been two bridges over the Falls, and George Washington Wilson photographed both. The first bridge was a wooden one – "an elegant rustic bridge," the writer James Brown called it in his *Guide to Deeside (the historian Joseph Robertson)* in 1831, and it certainly had a good deal more charm than its metal successor. Wilson photographed it in 1857 and the picture was used by Queen Victoria to make a sketch for her *Leaves from the Journal of our Life in the Highlands.*

The second bridge, whose construction is regarded as something of an engineering

feat, was built by Blaikie Brothers, Aberdeen, in 1878, the year in which Queen Victoria bought Ballochbuie Forest from Colonel James Ross Farquharson of Invercauld. Wilson's photograph was taken from virtually the same spot as his picture of the wooden bridge.

It appears at first glance to be a bridge to nowhere. The route by the Falls is said to be an ancient right-of-way. A barely discernible footpath follows it up the burn and along what was known as the Smuggler's Shank to Glen Doll and Glen Clova. Whisky smugglers went this way, car-

rying their illicit liquor over the hills on horseback. Now the old trail is followed only by the occasional hill-walker.

Downstream, there is actually another bridge over the Garbh-allt, a small wooden bridge seldom seen by sightseers. Below the falls there was a fog-house from which visitors could watch the cascading water. The name comes from the old Scots word "foggit," meaning covered with moss, and they were generally small garden summer-houses built or lined with mossy turf. The remains of a fog-house can still be seen in the Pass of Ballater.

Invercauld, "castle" on the Dee

INVERCAULD HOUSE, BRAEMAR FROM S.E.

When is a castle not a castle? From the Lion's Face rock on the south side of the River Dee, where George Washington Wilson took the picture below, the impressive mansion of Invercauld looks as much a castle as any of its rivals on Deeside.

Most people call it Invercauld House, as Wilson did in captioning his close-up of the building – "Invercauld House, Braemar, from S.E."

Some writers, however, have elevated it to castle rank. Dr Cuthbert Graham, in his "Portrait of Aberdeen and Deeside," described it as the Castle of Invercauld. "It is really a castle," he said.

The building, which incorporates part of the Farquharson stronghold dating back to the 16th century, began to take its present shape in the 17th century.

INVERCAULD. FROM THE LION'S FACE ROCK. 9. G.W.W.

Two Muckle Stanes

– they lie within a stone's throw of each other

"BIG STONE OF CLUNY." 36. E.C.

A.U.L. D1210

Two Muckle Stanes – and each with a tale to tell. It could be said that they are – or were within a stone's throw of each other. The stone in the top picture is the one which got Sandy Davidson, the famous poacher, into trouble with the Invercauld factor when it blocked a load of timber being floated down the Dee from Glen Derry. Sandy saved the factor's life, but got small thanks for it (see story on Page 28).

The stone in the lower picture is well-known to travellers going up Deeside to Braemar. It's called the Muckle Stane of Clunie and it lies in a field near the main road, not far from the Invercauld Bridge. It was said at one time to be "fairy-haunted."

Fairy-haunted or not, the Muckle or Meikle Stane was part of Creag Clunie, which rises above the road on its south side.

This huge rock is said to have broken away from the crag and hurtled down on to the road, bouncing across it and coming to rest on the north side.

The stone was also known as Erskine's Stone, for it marked the boundary between the Erskines of Clunie and Ballochbuie and the Farquharsons of Invercauld. The Erskines were claimants to the Earldom of Mar.

There are still quaint old cottages to be seen around Braemar, but visitors will look in vain for a dwelling like the one above. George Washington Wilson entitled it simply "Highland Cottage, Braemar." It is a cry-back to the days before Braemar became fashionable. Writing at the turn of the century, A. I. McConnochie described it as being at one time "the meanest of Highland clachans." It had "low, smokey, thatched, straggling buildings, overgrown with grass and noisesome weeds," he wrote. "There was but one inn, 'more suitable for drovers and excise officers than any higher description of travellers'." Did Wilson place the barrow strategically for his photograph, or did its owner flee before he pressed the button?

A coach and four at the old Inver Inn. It was known as the Invercauld Arms.

On the Braes o' Mar

AUCHENDRYNE, FROM MORRONE. 10,151. G.W.W.

A.U.L. A1679

The Braes o' Mar . . . the lovely setting of Deeside's most famous village. Here, thousands of people from all over the world gather every year for the Braemar Gathering. They are drawn, not only by its spectacle, but by the fact that the Queen and members of the Royal Family are regular attenders.

The Gathering took place at various sites last century, including Balmoral, but George Washington Wilson's picture, taken from Morrone, shows the present site in Auchendryne (lower left of picture). The Duke of Fife gifted the ground – a 12-acre site known as Moin-a-Gail – in 1905 as a permanent arena for the Games. It is now called the Princess Royal and Duke of Fife Memorial Park.

In the middle distance can be seen Braemar Castle, while to the left of it, on the opposite side of the River Dee, is a granite obelisk erected to the memory of James Farquharson of Invercauld, who died in 1862.

How a Deeside village was split in two

BRAEMAR, FROM MORRONE. 13,021. G.W.W.

A.U.L. A92

● **See overleaf**

ROYAL BRAEMAR . . .

The village of Braemar was at one time two separate communities – Castleton of Braemar and Auchendryne. How this came about, and the fierce rivalry that existed because of it, is described in the following pages. The picture below shows Auchendryne, to the west of the Water of Clunie. The Clunie, seen in Wilson's picture winding its way through the village, was the dividing line. Like the photograph on the previous page, this view was taken from Morrone.

. . . DIVIDED VILLAGE

The Castleton of Braemar – the other half of the village on the east bank of the Clunie. The name "Castleton" comes from the old castle of Kindrochit, whose ruins can be seen near the bridge over the Clunie. Wilson toiled up two hills with his cumbersome equipment to get his bird's eye views of Braemar. As well as the pictures taken from Morrone, he also produced a number showing the village from the top of Craig Coynach, seen in the picture below.

A.U.L. A92

BRAEMAR
Public Hall, Reading Room, and Library,
WITH LAWN TENNIS COURT ADJOINING.

The sketch on the left headed the subscription list when plans were made to build the Victoria Hall in Braemar. The final result is seen in the picture above.

There was an introductory note to the list pointing out that "the most desirable site in the Village has been kindly granted by Colonel Farquharson, of Invercauld" for the building of the hall.

The Colonel's name headed the list with a donation of £100, while those of his friends followed on, including two subscribers from Scarborough, one with £50, the other with a more modest £10.5s. The estimated cost of the hall was about £2000.

Heading the list were the words "Braemar Public Hall, Reading Room, and Library, with lawn tennis court adjoining," but at present it is used for a different purpose.

The name "Victoria Hall," seen above the entrance, has been covered over with a board saying "Invercauld Galleries." Here, Mrs Farquharson, wife of the laird, Capt. A. A. C. Farquharson of Invercauld, has run exhibitions of craftwork and paintings.

The hall in Auchendryne.

R.S.

"What's going on?" asked the Duke

– and up went hall No. 2

The Duke of Fife was travelling along the old military road in Braemar when he looked over to the Castleton and saw work being done above the east bank of the Water of Clunie. He told his driver to stop the coach. "What's going on there?" he asked.

"They're building a new hall for the Jubilee of the Queen," said the coachman.

"Oh, are they," said the Duke. "Drive on!"

Next day, on the Duke's instructions, work was started on a new Jubilee hall on the west bank of the Clunie – in Auchendryne.

That, they say, is how Braemar came to have two Victoria Halls, one on the approach to the village from the Cairnwell, the other on the road leading out of the village to Mar Lodge.

Braemar was – and, in some respects, still is – a divided village. It has two distinct communities, separated by the Clunie – Castletown, which is on Farquharson of Invercauld's estate, and Auchindryne, which was built on the property of the Duke of Fife. The hall incident illustrates what one 19th century writer called the "competitive struggle" between the two lairds.

"The village, situated on both banks of Clunie Water, is double – each portion jealous of its individuality," wrote Alex Inkson McConnochie in 1898. "No small rivalry exists between the east and west sides of the Clunie."

"LUDICROUS"

Another Deeside writer, Robert Anderson, said the rivalry had been carried on "with ludicrous results," while John Mackintosh probably alienated his readers in Auchendryne by describing Castletown as the capital of Braemar, although it is true that the name is now often used to mean the whole of the village.

Braemar not only has two halls – each community also has its own hotel. The Invercauld Arms, which lies in Castletown, greets the visitor arriving from Ballater, but cross the Cluny Bridge to Auchendryne and you have the Fife Arms.

The Roman Catholics lived in Auchendryne and the Protestants in Castletown. If the rivalry ever went beyond words, the lairds had their own armies ready for battle – the Duff Highlanders (Duff is the Fife family name) and the Farquharson Highlanders.

The name Auchendryne is from the Gaelic *Ach an Droighinn*, meaning "field of the thorn," but relationships between the rival communities are less prickly now than they once were. The folk in Auchendryne have even been showing a new-found interest in the Victoria Hall in Castletown.

In recent years, however, the hall has become better known as the Invercauld Galleries. Here, Mrs Farquharson, wife of Captain A.A.C. Farquharson of Invercauld, has organised exhibitions of craftwork and paintings. Some people, however, feel that the hall should revert to its original function – as a public hall.

CLUNY MILL

George Washington Wilson photographed the Victoria Hall in Castletown, but doesn't appear to have turned his camera on its wooden counterpart in Auchendryne. Despite that, G.W.W. pictures have been on show at exhibitions held in the hall in recent years.

In 1870, Wilson photographed the Mill of Auchendryne – the Mill on the Cluny – from the bridge that divides Castletown and Auchendryne. A copy of the photograph hangs inside the mill, which means that John Duff can see a picture of the mill as well as the real thing. John, a retired police officer, who was well-known as leader of the first Braemar mountain rescue team, has spent his retirement renovating the old mill, which is now his home.

FIFE ARMS GOES UP

Braemar boasts two hotels . . . one in Castleton, the other in Auchendryne. The picture on left shows work going ahead on the building of the Fife Arms Hotel. It was an imposing building, but it was to change considerably over the years.

The Fife Arms in George Washington Wilson's time. The passing of one era and the coming of a new one is signalled in Wilson's picture. Outside the entrance of the hotel a coach and four waits to pick up its passengers, while farther along the road a smart omnibus is ready to begin its run to Ballater. The ominibuses carried sixteen passengers inside and two on the seat alongside the driver.

99

ELEGANT LADIES' DRAWING-ROOM

The Invercauld Arms Hotel, competing with the Fife Arms round the corner, claimed that it had the "finest hotel situation in Scotland."

The hotel advertised coaches during the season to Blairgowrie, Dunkeld and Ballater. The omnibuses ran a popular "Three Rivers Tour," started in June, 1907. There were close links with the Great North of Scotland Railway and the railway company operated a station and office behind the Invercauld Hotel.

In the advertisement on left, the hotel promoted its "large dining hall, elegant ladies' drawing room, a billiard room and a smoking room."

BRAEMAR.

INVERCAULD ARMS HOTEL

(In connection with the Invercauld Arms Hotel, Ballater).

THE FINEST HOTEL SITUATION IN SCOTLAND.

Recently Re-erected after Plans by J. T. WIMPERIS, Esq., Sackville St., London.

LARGE DINING-HALL, ELEGANT LADIES' DRAWING-ROOM, BILLIARD-ROOM, SMOKING-ROOM, AND NUMEROUS SUITES OF APARTMENTS.

POSTING IN ALL ITS BRANCHES.

COACHES DURING THE SEASON TO
BLAIRGOWRIE, DUNKELD, AND BALLATER.

LETTERS AND TELEGRAMS PUNCTUALLY ATTENDED TO.

ALEX. McGREGOR.

FIFE CLANSMEN MARCHING TO THE

A.U.L. D2135

The March of the Clansmen

"There were gleams of sunshine, which, with the Highlanders in their brilliant and picturesque dresses, the wild notes of the pipes, the band, and the beautiful background of mountains, rendered the scene wild and striking in the extreme . . ."

So wrote Queen Victoria after the Braemar Gathering of September, 1859. There were three "armies" at the Gathering; as the Queen noted, there were "the Farquharson's men, headed by Colonel Farquharson, the Duff's by Lord Fife, and the Forbes's men by Sir Charles Forbes."

Despite the rivalry between the Farquharsons and the Duffs, there was little likelihood of a clan battle. "The Deeside Highlanders of today," wrote Robert

Anderson in 1911, "have no resemblance to the old clansmen, except perhaps in the matter of dress; certainly they do not imitate their manners or their methods.

"They are still in a sense, but a very modified sense, the 'retainers' of their respective lairds, being their tenants or employees; but they own no tribal fealty or clan service, and they assemble only on

ceremonial occasions, chiefly at the annual Gathering."

Still, they look an impressive lot in Washington Wilson's photograph . . . and one nervous lady lifts her skirts and steps delicately to the side as the brawny Highlanders come sweeping down the road, pipes blowing, flags flying, halberts on their shoulders.

101

MILL ON THE CLUNY. BRAEMAR. I. G.W.W.

A.U.L. C2794

Seeing double!

John Duff sees "double" when he looks at this view.

George Washington Wilson's photograph of the old Mill of Auchendryne hangs in his home, but John only has to step outside to see the real thing.

For John, a retired police officer and the leader of the first Braemar mountain rescue team, bought the old mill on the Clunie and made it his home. He calls it the Granary and for the past few years has been busy restoring it.

The original mill wheel is still in tact. John is seen on right working on the wheel.

The Water of Clunie is the boundary line between Auchendryne and Castletown.

R.S.

John Duff one of the pioneers of the mountain rescue service on Deeside, seen at the old wheel which he is restoring at his home at the Mill of Auchendryne.

LINN OF CORRYMULZIE, BRAEMAR. 10.158. G.W.W.

A.U.L. A93

The Falls of Corriemulzie, three miles from Braemar. Water from the Corriemulzie stream was harnessed to supply heating and lighting for New Mar Lodge, which stood near the falls. See opposite page.

New Mar Lodge at Corriemulzie.

A.U.L. CI023

They set off for the torchlight ball at seven o'clock in the evening. The Queen wore a white bonnet and had a plaid scarf slung over her shoulder, while the Prince Consort was in Highland dress. When they arrived at their destination they were taken to a curtained space where a board 100ft. long and 60ft. wide had been laid out.

"It was really a beautiful and most unusual sight," wrote Queen Victoria. The dance board was entirely surrounded by Highlanders carrying torches. There were seven pipers, playing together. Three Highlanders danced a reel holding torches in their hands.

ROMANTIC BALL

The venue for this romantic torchlight ball, which took place in September, 1852, was Corriemulzie Cottage, which was later renamed New Mar Lodge. The word "New" marked it out from the first Mar Lodge, a plain-looking building, which stood on the north side of the river Dee almost on the site of the present Mar Lodge.

New Mar Lodge, which was built in the middle of the 18th century and originally owned by the Mackenzie family, was the summer

When the Queen danced at Corriemulzie

home of the Earl of Fife, who married Princess Louise and in 1900 became the first Duke of Fife.

Not everyone was complimentary about it. One writer said it made "no pretention to being more than a Highland shooting box." But, as can be seen from the picture above, the setting was superb, for it stood on he wooded slopes of Creag an Fhitich.

In 1895, New Mar Lodge was destroyed by fire. It was decided to build another lodge on the north side of the Dee, virtually on the site of the demolished Old Mar Lodge, and in October, 1895, the foundation stone was laid by Queen Victoria.

The Princess Royal, whose marriage to the Earl of Fife in 1889 was

described by the Queen as "brilliant" – "he is immensely rich," she wrote – drew the first rough sketch.

Today, the third Mar Lodge is known to thousands of visitors to Deeside – and to wealthy guests who come from abroad to shoot over the 75,000-acre estate.

SKI PLANS

In 1961, it was bought by Swiss businessmen Gerald and John Panchaud, who also owned sporting estates in North Harris and Moray. Their aim was to turn it into a winter ski development, but lack of snow in the first two years of the project put paid to their plans.

For a time it was run as a luxury hotel, and in recent years the main

guests have been European sportsmen. John Panchaud died a number of years ago and Gerald died in May, 1989, a few months after selling the estate.

The new owner of Mar Lodge is an American billionaire, John Kluge (pronounced Kloogy), who already owns a 12,000-acre estate in Charlottesville, Virginia. Kluge, who is the second richest man in the United States, is thought to have paid between £5 million and £7 million for the Mar Lodge Estate.

When news of the purchase was announced, the quality Sunday newspaper colour magazines, taking a leaf from the book of the more sensational tabloid newpapers, homed in on the fact that Kluge's wife, Patricia, a 37-year-old Englishwoman, was a former London dancer. She married John Kluge, who is 34 years older, in 1981.

Deeside folk, who have learned to be cautious in what they say about their Royal neighbours, are likely to be no less tight-lipped about the new Laird of Mar Lodge and his wife. They will reserve judgement on the Kluges, who have taken over an estate, rich in tradition, that lies less than ten miles down the road from the gates of Balmoral Castle.

"Old Mar" – first of the Lodges

These unique photographs show the first of the three Mar Lodges built on upper Deeside. It stood on a site just to the rear of the present Mar Lodge.

Old Mar Lodge was a plain building by comparison with its successors, but its simplicity gave it a certain charm.

In the picture below, Duff Highlanders are seen mustering outside Old Mar Lodge in readiness for marching to the Braemar Gathering.

Save the stags' heads!

New Mar, which was originally called Corriemulzie Cottage, was a much more elaborate affair than its predecessor. Like the present Mar Lodge, which was once disparagingly described as "suburban Tudor," the "New" lodge came in for a good deal of criticism. One writer called it a "shapeless old hunting lodge with verandahs supported by rustic tree-trunks creosoted black," and the picture on right shows that he wasn't too wide of the mark.

The roofs were decorated with stags' heads (see picture below) and these were the pride and joy of the Duke of Fife. The lodge was burned down in 1895 and when the Duke was told it was ablaze he is said to have cried, "Save the stags' heads!"

A.U.L. C3987

A.U.L. F3982

The present Mar Lodge

Above – The third Mar Lodge as seen and photographed by George Washington Wilson a century ago. There have been changes to the building since then, but it is still recognisably the Mar Lodge that todays visitors see from the south bank of the River Dee on their way to the Linn of Dee.

Right – The entrance to Mar Lodge as it is today.

R.S.

A.U.L. F5472

Little and Muckle Inverey

There are two Invereys – Little Inverey and Meikle or Muckle Inverey. They are, in fact, two parts of the same village, separated by the Water of Ey. At one time, they were known as Wester Inverey and Easter Inverey.

When John Mackintosh wrote his "History of the Valley of the Dee" in 1895, he said there were twelve houses in Muckle Inverey. Most of them had been erected not long before he wrote the book; some were slated, but three or four of the old thatched ones still remained.

There was about the same number of houses in Little Inverey, five of which were thatched, four or five slated, and some of the others in ruins.

From Inverey, Glen Ey runs south to Beinn Iutharn. It is a lonely, deserted glen, its ruined holdings giving an almost haunted atmosphere to the valley. The inhabitants were ejected from their homes about 1840 to make way for deer. A ruined shooting lodge, Altanour, is at the head of the glen, hemmed in by skeleton-like trees, which add to the eeriness of the place.

Betty Allan, in her poem "Glen Ey Clearance," dismissed the idea that Glen Ey was desolated and a wilderness. "This dear place held our home and our happiness," she wrote. "Gleann mo chriddhe, my heart's desire!" Her poem told of the days when peat stacks were high and there were hinds for the taking and meal in the girnel.

"Warm the June sun on the hay at Aucherie," went her poem, but today Aucherie is a rickle of stones at the roadside.

Mackintosh said that eight families once lived in the glen. In the summer of 1893, he saw cattle grazing opposite the Colonel's Bed on the east side of the glen. The Colonel's Bed is where John Farquharson of Inverey hid after the Battle of Killiecrankie. His castle was in Muckle Inverey.

At one time, Inverey Cottage, occupied by the Duke of Fife's forester, was the only building at the entrance to the glen. Today, an imposing shooting lodge stands there.

Meikle Inverey is still very much as it was when George Washington Wilson took the picture above. The roofs of Mar Lodge can be seen across the River Dee, thrusting above the tree tops.

Two of Upper Deeside's best known characters had links with the buildings in the centre of the picture – see overleaf.

Tea, scones – and a dram

From the hostess at Thistle Cottage

Thistle Cottage.

Four hundred years have now
wheeled round,
With half a century more,
Since this has been
the burying ground
Belonging to the Gruers.

These lines in a Braemar kirkyard, commemorating the death in 1807 of a man called James Gruar, show that there have been Gruers on Deeside for many years. Some came over the old Monega Pass from Glen Isla to settle in the area. One was brutally stabbed to death by cateran in Caenlochan, and so much blood flowed that the spot became known as Grewar's Gutter.

The name is spelt in different ways, but to hundreds of walkers and climbers who tramped the Deeside hills in the years before the last war there was only one Gruer – the legendary Maggie Gruer, who took them in and gave them tea and scones and a "wee drap Glenlivet" if they were ill. They stayed at her home at Thistle Cottage in Inverey, where they were charged a shilling for bed and breakfast and a sixpence if they were hard up. Maggie kept the money in an enamel bucket.

"Hae ye pit yer name in my book?" she would ask. The names that went into the visitors' book included those of the poet Charles Murray; Henry Alexander, later Sir Henry, Lord Provost of Aberdeen, who wrote "The Cairngorms;" the playwright Robert Kemp; and Eric Linklater, the author. They were fed on home-made oatcakes and thick scones, which were Maggie's speciality, and when they left in the morning one satisfied customer wrote –

If I perish in the Pass, at least
I'll perish knowing,
That when I died I had inside
the nicest breakfast going.

Thistle Cottage can be picked out in George Washington Wilson's picture of Muckle Inverey (Little Inverey is on the other

The Barn.

side of the Ey Burn), but it was Maggie's mother who was there when he set up his tripod. Maggie's father, James Gruer, worked the croft behind the cottage and Mrs Gruer often gave a bed to passing hill-walkers, setting the pattern which her daughter followed for so many years.

Maggie was three when Wilson and George Walker visited Inverey. Walker said that the village was "formerly a collection of rude hovels." There is nothing to show that the two travellers were invited into Thistle Cottage to taste one of the famous Gruer scones.

Inverey has changed little since Maggie's day, or, indeed since Wilson took his picture of the hamlet, which is about two miles from the Linn o' Dee. In Wilson's time the road was not much more than a footpath. His picture shows that there were houses on the opposite side of the road.

Thistle Cottage is now a holiday home. Maggie would have been pleased to hear that, for at one time there was an attempt to stop the people of Inverey from taking in boarders. Maggie, who was not much of a letter-writer, got someone to write it for her and sent it to the Press. It was

read out in the House of Commons and Maggie said that when the King heard about it "he fairly danced."

"I held my heid fu' high," she said, when the objections were withdrawn.

Behind the cottage is the barn where weary climbers bedded down when the cottage was full up. It was also used for dances – up till some thirty years ago local organisations still held dances in Maggie Gruer's barn. Looking at it now, there seems hardly enough room to swing a cat, yet between fifty or sixty people – ghillies, crofters, maids, shepherds – crowded into it and "hooched" their way into the night. The "postie" provided the music on his fiddle and Maggie provided the refreshment – at threepence a head.

She was never backward at asking for her dues. "Tak' yer han' across yer pocket," she would say bluntly.

Maggie Gruer died in 1939 at the age of seventy-seven. People who remember her still talk nostalgically about her scones and butter, about the ever-ready teapot, and about the box bed into which Maggie climbed, fully clothed, while some of her guests

lingered at the fireside to talk about their day in the hills. "Scones?" read an entry in her visitors' book. "In loving memory!"

Ode to Maggie Gruer

Here's a rhyme to Maggie Gruer,
Inverey, ayont Braemar,
Fae gaed shelter to the hill folk
as they cam' fae near and far;
Fa put her' into the hiker when
his sark was gettin' damp,
For she'd aye a cheery welcome to
the fellow on the tramp.

When ye'd plytered through the
Lairig and ye looked an unco sicht,
Or ye'd peched and tyauved and
trachled owre Macdhui's steeny hicht,
And ye felt jist fair forfochen and
ye kent nae whaur to camp,
Oh, a bed at Maggie Gruer's was
sae welcome on the tramp!

The boy who became a legend

If Maggie Gruer was a legendary figure, the same could be said of Bob Scott. What Thistle Cottage and Maggie Gruer were to pre-war climbers and hill-walkers, the Luibeg bothy and Bob Scott were to the post-war generation of hill folk.

The bothy stood beside his keeper's cottage at Luibeg. Like Maggie, Bob was strict about his charges for overnight travellers. He always charged one shilling, but when decimalisation came in he increased it to 10p, arguing that that was only ten pence.

There are stories about how he chased defaulters up Glen Derry in his Land Rover.

Bob was educated at the Inverey Church of Scotland School, now a private house. Mrs Betty Lobban, who lives there, has a class photograph showing him in a high-buttoned jacket and a stiff white collar.

In the picture are (standing, left to right) Jeannie Smith, Ian Grant, William Gray, William Smith, Ella McLaren, Bob Scott and his sister Norah Scott. Front row – Marjory McLaren, Ethel McLaren, Miss Milne (teacher), and Dolly Anderson. One pupil, Walter Scott, is not in the picture.

Bob Scott retired in the early 1970's and went to live at the Quoich. He has now, as one writer put it, "gone to the great hill in the sky."

Mrs Betty Lobban's house at the Old School.

110

"THE GALLOWS TREE." MAR LODGE. 2485. G.W.W.

The Hanging Tree as G.W.W.'s camera captured it, still green and flourishing as the prophecy predicted. Today, a century on, it is a bare and lifeless trunk (see right), held upright by steel wires.

111

R.S.

The sleepy village of Inverey seems an unlikely place for ghosts and gallows trees, but myth and legend lurk behind the row of cottages on the road from Braemar to the Linn o' Dee. When Wilson and Walker were here they had a look at a ruin not far from Maggie Gruer's cottage. "In the centre of the village," wrote Walker, "an old wall of thirty feet in height, with some slits and narrow windows, is all that remains of the Castle of Inverey, the seat of a freebooter, Farquharson."

Even then, few people noticed the castle, or what was left of it, and fewer notice it now. It lies behind the derelict building, Albany Cottage, next to Maggie Gruer's house. West of that is the Mains, which was once occupied by Charlie Stuart, known as the King of Inverey. Maggie was the Queen.

I have heard stories about an underground tunnel running from the castle to Charlie Stuart's house, or from the older houses that once stood behind it, but no one has ever unearthed it. Still, it wouldn't be surprising, for the Farquharson who lived in the castle was often on the run. He was John Farquharson of Inverey, better known as the Black Colonel.

The Black Colonel lived at a time when Clan Farquharson dominated the countryside from the Wells of Dee to Cromar. They made their own laws and they thought nothing of "lifting" Lowlanders cattle. The Inverey Farquharsons, like other Highland lairds, had a Gallows Tree for handing out rough justice to people who disagreed with them. It can still be seen just west of the bridge – Victoria Bridge – leading to Mar Lodge.

When the Invercauld Farquharsons hanged an Inverey man on his own Gallows Tree for some minor offence, his mother is said to have cursed the clan and predicted the downfall of the Farquharsons –

The tree will flourish high and broad,
Green as it grows today,
When from the banks o' bonnie Dee
Clan Fionnladh's all away.

The direct male line did die out, but another part of the prophecy has fallen away. The Gallows Tree at Inverey is neither flourishing nor green. Washington Wilson's picture shows it "high and broad," full of foliage, but today it has become a lifeless trunk, rotting away and held up only by steel wires.

John Farquharson made his mark in history through "The Baron of Brackley," a ballad that confuses two different events. One was the murder of the Baron of Brackley in 1592 by cateran, the other was a clash in 1666 between John Gordon of Brackley and John Gordon of Inverey.

COLONEL'S CAVE

The Castle of Inverey was burned to the ground by Royal troops after the Battle of Killiecrankie in 1715. Mrs Elizabeth Lobban, who, lives in the Old Schoolhouse at Inverey, pointed out a huge rock on top of Creag a' Chait, a hill beyond the village. Up there, she told me, was the Colonel's Cave, where John Farquharson is said to have watched his castle going up in flames.

The Colonel's Cave is less well-known than the Colonel's Bed in Glen Ey. Here, where a track runs

When the Black Colonel rode

south to the crumbling remains of Altanour Lodge, lying in the shadow of the "mountains of hell", Beinn Iutharn Mhor and Beinn Iutharn Bheag. Farquharson found shelter in a narrow, rocky gorge on the Ey Burn.

His hiding-place has been a tourist attraction for many years. It is a lovely spot, as Washington Wilson's photographs show, but at times it can be slippery and dangerous. The "bed" is a recess on a rocky ledge; if the Colonel had fallen out of it he would have landed in a deep, black pool.

They say that from time to time he shared his "bed" with his mistress, Annie Bhan, who later died and was buried in Inverey churchyard.

Walker described in detail how he went with Wilson to photograph the Colonel's Bed. They rode part of the way in a dog-cart, but had to stop at the nearest farm – "not being allowed to proceed farther for the chance of meeting his Lordship's vehicle on the narrow road." Nowadays, unless you have permission, cars are banned, although the track is wide enough to take two-way traffic, a development that angered conservationists.

COLONEL'S BED

"Descending by a footpath which

the feet of numerous pilgrims had formed, we reached the Colonel's Bed, a large long fissure in the rock under beetling precipices which approached so closely above as almost to exclude the light of day," wrote Walker.

Wilson took some shots in which the light, streaming around the edges of the rock, "had a very peculiar effect" (see Page 116). Photography in those pioneering days wasn't quite the same as it is today. It required special skills and endless patience – and strong nerves! Walker, describing their work at the Colonel's bed, spoke about "the exciting character of taking photographic pictures." "Talk of deer-stalking!" he said. He thought it was a bit like hunting stags or gaffing salmon.

There is an eerie postscript to the story of the Black Colonel. When he died, he left instructions that he should be buried beside Annie Bhan in Inverey churchyard, not far from the ruined Castle of Inverey. His relatives wanted him laid to rest in the family burial ground at Castletown of Braemar, but every time they put him there his corpse was found next morning lying above the ground. It happened again and again, and eventually his widow agreed that the body should be transferred to Inverey.

From here he watched his castle burn . . .

The stones in the picture on right are all that is left of the old graveyard where the Black Colonel was buried.

From it you can look west to Creag a' Chait, where a huge rock formation juts out above the woodlands across the Water of Ey. This is the Colonel's Cave, from which John Farquharson of Inverey watched Government troops burn his castle to the ground.

The picture on the opposite page shows the view from the Colonel's Cave today . . . the road to Linn o' Dee running through the village, Mar Lodge in the distance, and in the centre of the picture the shooting lodge erected at the mouth of Glen Ey in recent years.

The ruins of the Castle of Inverey stand in a clump of trees on the north side of the road, where a caravan can be seen.

114

"A wild and dreary region," was how Washington Wilson's companion, George Walker, described Glen Ey, a place "where the streams tumbled down the faces of the hill making sheer leaps of hundreds of feet at a bound." They were there to photograph the Colonel's Bed, where John Farquharson of Inverey hid out when hunted by Government troops. This was one of the pictures Wilson took with equipment which they carried down the dangerous gorge on their backs.

A.U.L. C5722

This picture of the Colonel's Bed was one of the views which George Walker said was "taken in the gloom in which the light, streaming round the edge of the rock, had a very peculiar effect." They waited anxiously for the sun to "gild the tips of the rocks, lighten the foreground with a living glory, and stamp the picture as 'a joy forever'." They got their picture, climbed to the top, and "trudged down the glen in high spirits."

116

Loch Callater and Glenshee

When George Washington Wilson explored Deeside with his cameras, they ranged beyond the limits of the valley, over the Cairnwell to the Spittal of Glenshee (see right and opposite page) and into the long and lonely reaches of Glen Callater.

Loch Callater (above) lies three miles south of the farm of Auchallater on the main Braemar road. There is a deserted lodge on the edge of the loch, where a path winds along the water's edge and climbs over the Tolmount and Jock's Road before dropping down to Glen Doll.

In winter, this old Mounth route is swept by storms. In the New Year of January, 1959, five Glasgow men were lost on the plateau when they set out to cross the Tolmounth Pass and ran into a raging blizzard.

There is a metal plaque to their memory on a stone near a bothy on Jock's Road.

On the edge of Loch Callater, near the lodge, there is a large boul-der marking the site of the Priest's Well. The story goes that on one occasion the frost was so hard that the local people were unable to get water from the spring there. The priest prayed – and the well thawed.

The mountain overlooking the well is Carn an t-Sagairt, the Priest's Mountain, better known now as Cairn Taggart, which is in the Lochnagar range. There is also a loch, Loch Phadruig, which is said to be named after the priest (Peter).

The Spittal of Glenshee has bene-fited from the booming ski industry in recent years. Wilson's picture shows the Spittal hotel, set against its spectacularly beautiful moun-tain background.

Glen Shee is the longest and most important of the southern glens of the Grampians. The line formed by it and by Glen Clunie, which crosses the Cairnwell at a height of 2199 ft., has always been the main route linking the south country with Deeside.

The Spittal of Glenshee

The Spittal of Glenshee.

The Quoich – and the Earl's Punchbowl

The Falls of Quoich, which are about half a mile from the river Dee, are regarded by some people as being just as spectacular as the thundering waters of the Linn of Dee.

The big tourist attraction at the Quoich is the Earl of Mar's Punch-bowl, a huge pot-hole worn in the rock by eddying sand and pebbles. It got its name because of its shape – like a quaich or a cup.

Tradition says that it was called the Punch-bowl when the Earl of Mar raised the Jacobite standard at Braemar and brewed a monster bowl of punch in honour of his followers.

The Earl's punch-bowl sprung a leak a long time ago and it is generally hidden by the rushing Quoich Water.

Our picture on right caught it during a dry spell, when the water was unusually low, giving a first-class view of the bowl without its contents.

LINN OF DEE, BRAEMAR. 2. G.W.W.

A.U.L. C2795

The Linn of Dee marks the end of the public road for travellers going west through Deeside. Beyond that, dusty tracks spin off to the distant hills . . . to the Lairig Ghru, through Glen Tilt to Blair Atholl, and north by the Lairig an Laoigh to Speyside.

Hundreds of people come by coach and car each year to peer down at the Dee's turbulent waters from the bridge built at the Linn in 1857. Here, the river rushes through a narrow channel between 3ft. and 4ft. wide, then opens out into a series of round pools.

The granite bridge was opened by Queen Victoria on September 8, 1857. The ladies, Victoria noted in her diary, had only returned at five o'clock in the morning from a ball at Mar Lodge. The Royal party were dressed in what the Queen called "highland state" – Prince Albert in a Royal Stewart plaid and the girls in tartan skirts.

PIPERS PLAYING

Queen Victoria thought the valley of the Dee looked beautiful. "A triumphal arch was erected," she wrote, "at which Lord Fife and Mr Brooke received us, and walked near the carriage, pipers playing – the road lined with Duff men."

Washington Wilson and his faithful companion, George Walker, camped at the Linn of Dee during their photographic foray up Deeside. "Towards Castleton the clouds hung heavy and low and we could see that it poured," wrote Walker, "so, hurriedly erecting our tent on the rocky banks, we secured some records of our visit while the day kept up."

END OF THE ROAD

The striking picture above is from Wilson's "records" at the Linn.

"A handsome new stone bridge, with some character about it, opened by her Majesty, now spans the gorge a little to the west of where the old wooden structure stood," noted Walker. "The water was larger than we had ever seen it, and tinged with moss, telling of rain up in the glen."

Next day, the two men went to the Linn of Quoich to take pictures, but were drawn back to the Linn of Dee by the sunshine. "With the sunlight it might be better," said Walker.

"Roe-deer stood under the thickets with timid wondering gaze," he wrote. "A large bird of peculiar plumage was observed running in the wood, and as only a very partial view of it was had our eager fancies instantly set it down as a Capercurlzie, some broods of which were introduced into the district in the hopes of propagation; but a nearer approach to it revealed a very good specimen of a bird which has absolutely no English name."

Wilson and Walker had a second look at the bridge. "Opinions vary greatly regarding it." said Walker. "When expectation is high it disappoints – to us it appeared very interesting."

Walker said it was "no difficult feat to step across the fall to a lower ledge, but getting back wasn't so easy. "It has been done, it may be done again; and it may be advisable to show that the race is not degenerating in spirit or foolhardiness. Several instances have occured in which the attempt has proved fatal, the rush and fall of the waters stunning, and the deep pool retaining and unfortunate, without any possibility of assistance."

WILD DESPAIR

Deacon Alexander Robb, the Aberdeen poet, described in "A Deeside Jaunt" how a passenger on his coach, "puff'd up with self-conceit," jumped across the gap and then took fright when he had to jump back.

O, his shine was suddenly ta'en out,
When to jump back again he turn'd about,
Pale was his face, and white as drifted snow,
Haggard his look, his nether lip hung low,
O, when I saw his look o' wild despair,
I turned me roun' and I could glower nae mair.

While Robb was looking the other way, the piper in the party – Piper Archie – got hold of two boards and threw them across "the frightful span," after which the "stupid whelp" was helped back to safety.

The Deacon, obviously unnerved by the experience, helped himself to a few drams when he got back to Ballater. "I got oblivious," he said, "and mind naething mair."